NEW ARCHITECTURE IN CHINA

BERNARD CHAN

NEW ARCHITECTURE IN CHINA

MERRELL
LONDON · NEW YORK

First published 2005 by Merrell Publishers Limited

Head office:
81 Southwark Street
London SE1 0HX

New York office:
49 West 24th Street, 8th Floor
New York, NY 10010

www.merrellpublishers.com

Publisher Hugh Merrell
Editorial Director Julian Honer
US Director Joan Brookbank
Sales and Marketing Manager Kim Cope
Sales and Marketing Executive Nora Kamprath
Managing Editor Anthea Snow
Project Editor Claire Chandler
Junior Editor Helen Miles
Art Director Nicola Bailey
Junior Designer Paul Shinn
Production Manager Michelle Draycott
Production Controller Sadie Butler

Text copyright © 2005 Bernard Chan
Design and layout copyright © 2005 Merrell Publishers Limited
Illustrations copyright © 2005 the copyright holders; see p. 240

British Library Cataloguing-in-Publication Data:
Chan, Bernard
New Architecture in China
1.Architecture – China – 21st century
I.Title
720.9′51′0905

ISBN 1 85894 299 3

Project managed by Marion Moisy
Edited by Tom Neville

Printed and bound in China

ACKNOWLEDGEMENTS

I would like to offer special thanks to Hugh Merrell and Julian Honer for their faith and courage in commissioning me to take on this momentous and challenging task. I was first inspired to write this book while I was working as an editor at Pace Publishing Limited, and my appreciation goes to my ex-publisher. Thanks also to all the participants for submitting the materials on time and in the most professional manner. The research work was made enjoyable by the kind assistance of the staff at the Central Library next to the scenic Victoria Park, Hong Kong. Finally, I am grateful to my supporting team at p&d Editorial, in particular Anna Koor and Jeremy Siu, and – last but not least – to my beloved one for all the lost evenings and weekends.

Bernard Chan
Hong Kong, 2005

JACKET, FRONT
Bamboo House, Commune-By-The-Wall, Beijing, by Kengo Kuma, 2000–02 (see pp. 104–105)

JACKET, BACK
Plaza 66, Nanjing Xi Lu, Shanghai, by Kohn Pedersen Fox Associates, 1994–2001 (see pp. 208–209)

PAGE 2
Luyeyuan Stone Sculpture Art Museum, Xinmin, Chengdu, by Jiakun Architects, 2001–02 (see pp. 32–33)

CONTENTS

The 1800-seat Shanghai Grand Theatre was designed by French architect Jean-Marie Charpentier in 1998. With the extruded geometry of its square base and upward-curving roof, it is seen as a contemporary symbol of Chinese culture.

China's transformation over the last century has been well documented by researchers from both West and East. The superlatives applied to the country's urban development barely succeed in becoming familiar statistics – never mind clichés – before the figures are surpassed by yet another astonishing feat. However, the story of China's emergence as an architectural superpower is only in its infancy. Its flowering has been recent and dramatic rather than the result of a steady, gradual evolution. The origins of modern Chinese architecture can arguably only be traced back little more than a quarter of a century and, not surprisingly, its development has paralleled the country's growing role in the world's political and economic arenas.

At the start of the twentieth century, the building methods of traditional Chinese architecture largely followed the standards and guidelines laid down by manuals such as *Ying Tsao Fashi*, written in 1103. The German scholar Eduard Kögel cites the document's widespread use up to the 1911 revolution and the overturning of the imperial dynastic system of the last Ching dynasty (abstract of paper 'Search for Identity in Contemporary Architecture in China', delivered at Architecture and Identity conference in Berlin, 2004; www.architecture-identity.de). Even after that time, Chinese architecture continued to be influenced by the axial and hierarchical layout of Beijing's Forbidden City.

Kögel traces the return of China's first generation of overseas-trained architects in the 1920s, including figures such as Liang Sicheng, Xi Fuquan and Xia Changxi (Zhongshan Hospital, Guangzhou). Although strongly influenced by the Parisian Ecole des Beaux-Arts, the principles of Neo-classicism and the Modernist debate in Germany, their architectural pursuits back in their home country led them to search for typologies appropriate to China, both culturally and climatically. Kögel's research points to their desire to create a language that reflects local context; he cites early examples of work by Changxi as conveying an understanding of climatically responsive architecture.

In *Building in China – Henry K. Murphy's Adaptive Architecture, 1914–1935* (Hong Kong 2001), Jeffrey Cody examines the work of an American architect in China. Murphy visited during the First World War and developed a passion for historic Chinese architecture. He completed a number of large educational campus projects, increasingly incorporating features and motifs that he regarded as architecture with an 'Orientalist nature', though they remained Neo-classical in plan. Murphy may have prompted the beginnings of a movement that saw architects aspiring to design Western structures dressed in Oriental features in order to formulate a 'Chinese style'.

In his seminal text, 'In the Absence of Authenticity – An Interpretation of Contemporary Chinese Architecture' (*Nordisk Arkitekturforskning: Nordic Journal of Architectural Research*, vol. 8, no. 3, 1995), architecture critic Pu Miao maintains that the roots of Chinese contemporary architecture can be linked to the events of 1949, when the Communist Party took power. A further milestone in its evolution came in the wake of the large-scale economic reforms of 1978 onwards. Miao, like many others, believes that "contemporary Chinese architecture, as an art, has yet to develop a language specific to its own unique conditions".

During the 1950s China increasingly looked to the Soviet Union as its architectural role model. In Beijing, where the ancient city was already defined by gridded streetscapes, it smoothed the way towards industrialization and modernization. Architecture was targeted, alongside artistry and craftsmanship, as a dangerous form of bourgeois decadence. In order to maintain centralized control, the Communist Party placed architectural design in the hands of various state-owned 'design institutes', thereby ensuring that it became a tool of state policy, strictly upheld. The built environment played an important role in uniting the populace and projecting the image of a socialist China to the rest of the world. The significance of architecture in capturing the essence of the nation, its traditions, culture and aesthetic

The Great Wall Sheraton Hotel is located in the heart of Bejing's diplomatic quarter. Designed by US firm Ellerbe Becket, when built in 1983 it was China's first five-star hotel, its reflective glass curtain-walled façade projecting an appropriately international image.

values, was never underestimated. Building programmes conformed to the principles of 'national form, socialist content' promulgated by the Soviet Union.

During the decade-long Cultural Revolution launched by Mao Zedong in 1966, the architectural arts were largely suppressed. Many design institutes were closed, their architects and engineers sent to work the fields in the countryside. After Mao's death in 1976, city planning and building construction took a different direction. With the implementation of China's open-door policy in the 1980s, architects and designers were able to return to the cities and continue where they had left off. However, Western influence in the form of architectural exchange began to take root rapidly. The Chinese government designated Shenzhen a Special Economic Zone in 1979, inviting foreign investors to take advantage of access to cheap land and labour. Relaxation of restrictions had an enormous impact on the pace of change, fuelling a renaissance in all aspects of China's culture, including a belated interest in its unique heritage, much of which had been destroyed.

Miao uses Martin Heidegger's theory of authenticity to help understand China's approach to architecture. He provides a simplified definition: "Authentic architecture must actively seek forms which plainly express the true conditions of its users' social, cultural and economic life." Surveying numerous examples of what China considers high-profile architectural works – primarily those that have garnered the most awards and been most frequently published – Miao concludes that there are three general characteristics that can be applied to these buildings. First, the design strategy is based on imitation; secondly, the treatment of the building involves production of a 'false image'; thirdly, the appearance of the building is mannered, involving cosmetic decoration. He describes how Chinese architects adopt stylistic cues when confronted with different building typologies. 'Russian Classical' is applied to government buildings; cultural institutions and gardens are endowed with a 'Chinese Classical' language; Chinese vernacular is reserved for tourist facilities; and 'Western fashions' are borrowed for commercial and corporate developments. 'Modern' and 'Western' are often defined purely in terms of materials, hence the dominance of reflective glass curtain walls and exposed metal features.

The question of Chinese identity continued to dog politicians and architects through the 1980s. By the end of the decade, Shanghai's mayor, Zhu Rongji, had formulated his vision for a global city, and Pudong, an area covering 522 square kilometres to the east of the Huangpu River, became the focus of new urban development. Planning regulations in Beijing were, and still are, particularly stringent.

Building heights within a certain radius of the Forbidden City and Tiananmen Square are strictly curtailed. Reading through 'The Chronicle of Chinese Architecture: 1980–2003' (*Architecture and Urbanism*, Tokyo, no. 399, December 2003) compiled by architecture professor and critic Charlie Xue, it is clear where and how China's urban development accelerated. He reports that in 1983, under Deng Xiaoping, then chairman of the Communist Party, the country's state-run design institutes became self-supporting, no longer able to rely on government funds. The following year Deng welcomed the American president, Ronald Reagan, to China while endorsing the opening of fourteen coastal cities to international trade. Local architecture publications, such as *New Architecture* (Wuhan), and *Time + Architecture* (Shanghai), began to flourish. International conferences, exhibitions and symposia, hosted in Beijing, introduced local architects to Western expertise in the fields of building technology and computers as design tools. In 1987 Chinese architects participated in the Sixteenth Congress of the UIA (International Union of Architects), and Professor Wu Liangyong was elected vice chairman. The same year,

he embarked on an urban-renewal project in Beijing, leading a team from the Institute of Architectural and Urban Studies and the Architectural Design and Research Institute of Tsinghua University. The Ju'er Hutong development covers 8 hectares and revisits the traditional Chinese courtyard house. Where possible, existing buildings were restored and trees preserved, and the architects formulated a hierarchy of open, semi-open and private spaces.

With China welcoming the world with open arms, its tourism industry grew rapidly. The swelling numbers of business travellers from overseas, tapping into China's vast economy, fed the need for higher standards of urban amenities, particularly hotels and attractions such as galleries and museums. Xue draws parallels between China's changing political scene and major architectural achievements such as I.M. Pei's Fragrant Hill Hotel in Beijing. Built in 1982, the hotel was one of several early examples of the type, setting a benchmark in luxurious contemporary hospitality.

Pei is highly revered in China, and his biography follows a similar track to that of many young Chinese architects today.

Japanese architect Kisho Kurokawa designed the Chinese Japanese Youth Center in partnership with the Beijing Institute of Architectural Design in 1990. Jointly spearheaded by the former Japanese Prime Minister Yasuhiro Nakasone and the then Chinese Secretary Hu Yaobang, its architecture is inspired by a symbiosis of Japanese and Chinese cultures.

In 1934, aged 18, he left for the US to study architecture. According to Ulf Meyer in *Beijing, Shanghai, Shenzhen – Cities of the 21st Century* (Frankfurt 2000), Pei returned in 1974 as part of a delegation from the American Institute of Architects. On a lecture tour four years later he was offered the commission to design the Fragrant Hill Hotel: "He created an encapsulated, asymmetrical building with numerous inner courtyards. The structure, which is unobtrusively integrated into the landscape, embodies a modern reinterpretation of traditional Chinese spatial principles and ornamentation." The construction is described as relatively simple: it "cleverly links interior and exterior spaces and preserves tradition yet nonetheless introduces a contemporary style". Moreover, Meyer claims it represents a turning point in the debate over 'national form'.

At the Great Wall, Xue documents the construction of China's first curtain-wall building, the Great Wall Sheraton Hotel, designed by an American firm, Ellerbe Becket, in 1983. Such developments were not limited to the major cities. Special attention was also devoted to more remote tourist havens, such as Guilin in Guangxi Zhuang Autonomous Region and Qufu in Shandong Province. The Queli Guesthouse, designed in 1985 by Dai Nianci, then deputy minister of construction, is a telling example of what was considered sensitive and appropriate for Qufu, the birthplace of Confucius.

In his research, Miao hints at examples of where one might find authenticity in building methodology. He describes the architecture of traditional villages, houses and other everyday places as "straightforward, simple, solemn and heavy". He adds some further clues in the architecture's

"frank articulation of infill wall and framing system, in the strong dark timber beams and columns and the natural textures of brick and stone and the way the form of the sloped roofs is generated by the structure and function".

It is not as though architects building in China are insensitive to this issue. There are many examples of work that is inspired by the axial planning and formal hierarchy of family dwellings such as courtyard houses. The issues of solid and void, intricate variations in perspective – closed versus open, constriction then expansion – frequently inspire architects in their efforts to seek authenticity. Hong Kong architect Rocco Yim explores these phenomena in his recent book *Being Chinese in Architecture: Recent Works in China by Rocco Design* (Hong Kong 2004). As the title suggests, he asks what constitutes 'Chinese-ness'. In the book Yim reflects on a paper he delivered to the Arcasia Forum in 1989, noting that "in order to ponder the future of Asian (Chinese) architecture we have to come to terms with who the modern Asian (Chinese) is".

China's rich architectural and cultural heritage has been appropriated by politicians and property developers, whose ambitions to create something unique that can be critically evaluated as Chinese-ness have resulted in a wave of superficial style regulations. Many of Beijing's and Shanghai's modern commercial buildings were required to incorporate distinctive Chinese features. Government ministers insisted that architects defer to traditional emblems or motifs, and this was often accomplished by superimposing tiled, pitched 'hat' rooftops on otherwise glossy, curtain-walled towers. The resulting pastiche of styles unleashed across numerous Chinese cities changed

Pudong International Airport opened in 1999. Designed by Paul Andreu Architecte, its uplifting, wing-like roof forms signify Shanghai's emergent international status as a twenty-first-century world city.

Located in the modern financial hub of Pudong, at 421 metres and 88 floors, Jin Mao Tower is Shanghai's tallest skyscraper. The mixed-use development, which was built in 1998, incorporates the Grand Hyatt Hotel on its top floors. With its series of setback features, the tower is described by its architect, SOM, as recalling the forms of traditional Chinese pagodas.

the face of urban development during the 1990s, as the country's economy shifted into top gear. The debate probably reached its peak around 1995. Images of Chinese-style buildings clad in blue reflective glass and muscular Western-style towers donning minuscule gold hats leapt out of the pages of Asian architecture magazines. The Hong Kong-based journal *hinge* gauged the opinion of Hong Kong architects at the time, some of whom – bowing to pressure from Chinese clients – were reluctantly contributing to the tribe of confused forms. Professor Puay-peng Ho from the Chinese University of Hong Kong, quoted in *hinge* (vol. 23, January 1996), emphasized the importance of culture and the spirit of the age when designing in China, and the place for traditional architecture:

> There is a context for its form, for its decorations etc., and that whole set of contexts cannot be transplanted without analysing what it means in the broader scale. Architecture has to be holistic, it has to be in unity, or in coherence with itself, therefore if you just pull elements of the traditional vocabulary then you are going to misrepresent that element, you are just going to have a "hat" without any function.

Ho presented the analogy of English missionaries who wore Chinese dress with round hats; their Chinese identity went very little deeper than a cosmetic layer.

As foreign investment began to pour into Chinese cities in the 1990s, the spotlight was thrown on large-scale, gleaming commercial complexes. One of the more extreme examples, and a benchmark in Beijing, was the Oriental Plaza complex – a multiuse commercial, retail and hotel development that was funded by Hong Kong developer Li Ka Shing. Designed by Hong Kong-based P&T Architects and Engineers, it covers 800,000 square metres and was the largest single multipurpose complex structure in Asia when it was built in 1999. Its size and scale would not normally be a point of contention, but it was sited close to Tiananmen Square and the Forbidden City. Another prime location and close neighbour came under microscopic scrutiny in 1997, when the idea of a grand theatre for Beijing emerged. An international architectural competition was orchestrated, involving forty-four submissions from overseas and mainland architects. The winning design by Paul Andreu Architecte became mired in controversy as critics argued over its appropriateness as an important cultural symbol for the capital city and its lack of sensitivity to Beijing's extreme climate. Variously nicknamed 'the bubble' or 'the egg', after

seven years the National Grand Theatre of China is now nearing completion, having weathered a bumpy ride that saw construction suspended on a number of occasions.

New buildings whose architecture borrowed from traditional Chinese symbols, motifs or symmetry in planning continued to win favour with Chinese developers and government authorities. The Shanghai Center, completed in 1989 by American architect John Portman, provides a rigid juxtaposition of different geometric forms. His later design for the Bund Center, also in Shanghai, is emblazoned with a crown in the form of lotus petals – a highly revered flower in China.

Among successful examples of the era was the Chinese Japanese Youth Center in Beijing, designed in 1990 by Japanese architect Kisho Kurokawa, who is known for his brand of abstract symbolism. He collaborated with the Beijing Institute of Architectural Design, and the two established a close working relationship. The buildings form a collection of geometry – circular and square – that can be read in Chinese cosmological terms as, respectively, the sky and the earth. However, many other buildings are blatantly direct in their representational ambitions, such as the Shanghai Museum, by Xing Tonghe of the Shanghai Institute of Architectural Design & Research, clad in a pink granite shipped in from Spain. The building's circle-and-square composition represents heaven and earth but is also based on the form of an ancient Chinese bronze vessel, the arches supposedly resembling its handles. The museum

stands by no means alone in the manicured gardens of People's Square. The square is coloured by a melting pot of architectural forms that line its edges, from the 1998 Shanghai Grand Theatre by Jean-Marie Charpentier, to the Shanghai Urban Planning and Exhibition Center completed two years later, and the pyramidal tower of Tomorrow Square, by John Portman. In the words of Kögel, the square "testifies to a new concept of the city, one that combines cultural, administrative, historic and commercial dimensions". Despite the scorn poured on the architecture of the 468-metre-high Oriental Pearl TV Tower, its 'lollipop' form is a well-established icon that dominates Shanghai's Pudong skyline. Designed by the East China Architectural Design & Research Institute, it is intended to convey the image of two dragons playing with pearls – a string of steel spheres is stacked up its length.

The death of the economic reformer Deng Xiaoping in 1997 did not slow the pace of urban development, particularly in Shanghai. At that stage there were dozens of 'landmark' projects lined up on drawing boards to compete for centre-stage on the Pudong skyline. The 'Paris-of-the-East' image may well have been lost in Shanghai's quest to become number one city in greater China, threatening to overtake Hong Kong in both the economic and cosmopolitan stakes. Development has centred on the Lujiazhui Finance and Trade Zone; by the end of 1995 there were 181 high-rises under construction in this district alone, according to figures quoted in *hinge* magazine (vol. 30, March 1997). Key developments rising out of the ground

The five-storey Shanghai Urban Planning and Exhibition Center, designed by the East China Architectural Design & Research Institute, showcases a vision of urban development in the city. It became a symbol of the new millennium when it opened in the year 2000. The distinctive roof features are designed to emulate a magnolia, the city's flower.

The Renaissance Tianjin Teda Hotel and Convention Center was designed by Florida-based architects Wimberly Allison Tong & Goo on the site of a partially constructed building. It was completed in 2004. The façade largely owes its wave-like form to the principles of feng shui.

around the city included the Jin Mao Tower, Shanghai World Financial Center, Plaza 66 and the Shanghai Securities Exchange. At the time, architects expressed their concern over the coherency of Pudong's masterplan and the absence of a connected urban fabric. Today it is clear that they were right to be worried.

Approaching the end of the century, China had already fully embraced modernization, to the extent that large tracts of traditional urban fabric in cities such as Beijing and Shanghai had been razed to make way for modern, international-style skyscrapers. Many critics have been horrified by the indiscriminate demolition that has left few of the traditional *hutong* alleyways and courtyard houses. However, it was not long before one developer saw the economic benefits of preserving these neighbourhoods. Xintiandi in Shanghai was China's first example, formed in 2001 by restoring fifteen or so of the city's traditional *shikumen* houses and a former French colonial mansion. The network of pedestrianized streets, plazas and alleyways has spawned high-class restaurants, luxury boutiques and alfresco cafés.

Around the same time, in June 2001, I.M. Pei flew into Beijing for the opening of the Bank of China headquarters. Mark O'Neill, writing in the *South China Morning Post* on 26 June 2001, commented that: "It marks part of the rapid transformation of the skyline over central Beijing that has aroused mixed feelings among local people." He also reported that the rock that features in the internal garden

came from a protected national park in Yunnan, and that the 15-metre-high bamboo undertook a three-day journey from Hangzhou. More importantly, he revealed that it was the first building in China to be clad in travertine stone – 40,000 square metres of it from a single quarry.

The country's rapid urbanization also spawned a new species of architecture – the multiuse development – that other cultures are only now assimilating. In *Beijing, Shanghai, Shenzhen – Cities of the 21st Century*, Dutch architect Rem Koolhaas identifies the activity of shopping as a key common factor defining the Asian city, and, indeed, it is rare to find an urban architectural programme in China with no retail component. The nation gave birth to the multiuse commercial and residential complex, and it has since become a fertile architectural model.

These conglomerations of buildings – including office towers, apartments, a hotel and considerable retail and entertainment space – are practically cities in their own right. They have altered the once-human scale and proportion of China's cityscapes beyond recognition. Often constructed on isolated pockets of land, their immenseness has been criticized for fragmenting the structure of the city and creating disconnected islands of development. However, developers and architects of these complexes argue that they meet the needs of an expanding, sophisticated population whose work and leisure are relatively intertwined; this is evident at Tomorrow Square and Plaza 66 in Shanghai, or Jianwai Soho in Beijing.

The Center of Jade Culture in Wuhan was designed by Zhao Bing in 2002. Its plan is informed by Chinese calligraphy, underlining the architect's interest in iconic symbolism. However, it also serves a functional role in controlling general circulation through the museum.

Yet Beijing-based architect Yung Ho Chang has offered an alternative model. His work has been documented by French architects Laurent Gutierrez and Valerie Portefaix in *Yung Ho Chang: Atelier Feichang Jianzhu – A Chinese Practice* (Hong Kong 2003). His projects may not be of the same scale, but scale is not the issue here. "Yung Ho Chang refuses to move into a site without warning, instead he finds a discreet means of infiltration. This is not classical medicine or surgery but intervention by an acupuncturist who considers the body as a whole and makes an overall diagnosis of the problem", write Gutierrez and Portefaix. Chang plays by a different set of rules. "The work of FCJZ usually makes a departure from the typical issues of building, such as programme, site, space, material and construction. Instead the foundations begin from ventures into the concerns of city, landscape, tradition and culture", according to his company profile.

Koolhaas has commented at length on the specific nature of the Chinese city. In *Beijing, Shanghai, Shenzhen – Cities of the 21st Century*, he defines it as:

a city which has built up a large volume in a very short span of time, and which, because of that, does not possess the slowness which corresponds to both the traditional building process and to a certain model of its authenticity. Beyond a certain construction pace, this sort of authenticity is unavoidably sacrificed, even if everything is made of stone and authentic materials – and exactly therein lies the irony.

The principle that architecture in China should relate to local conditions is again gaining favour, albeit the architects use a more subtle, meaningful language than that of their predecessors. Kögel cites work such as the Tiantai Museum in Zhejiang Province by Wang Lu and the Luyeyuan Stone Sculpture Art Museum in Chengdu by Liu Jiakun as examples that "show different ways of combining the tradition of local typology with the new content and a new form according to the knowledge of local craftsmanship".

Pu Miao also demonstrated this approach in 2002 when he designed the Teahouse in Xiao-lang-di Dam Park in Henan. He rejected European Modernism in favour of an approach that acknowledges the realities of Chinese culture and technology. The Teahouse forms an integral part of a park, where visitors come to enjoy the largest dam on the Yellow River. Indoor and outdoor dining is woven into the landscape through terraced spaces connected by bridges, encouraging varied experiences of the surroundings.

There is a growing confidence, and an urgency, among mainland Chinese architects that the roots of a modern Chinese architecture can be unearthed. Practices such as MADA s.p.a.m. and Urbanus Architecture and Design, among others, are regarded as the forerunners of China's next generation. Established in 1999 by Qingyun Ma, MADA s.p.a.m. confronts the specific context of China, describing the country's speed of development and hunger for change as requiring an approach "where there are no boundaries between planning, architecture, landscape and media". Ma's background is typical of these emerging architectural talents: trained at Tsinghua University, he completed his masters at the University of Pennsylvania before practising in the US for a few years. He set up MADA s.p.a.m. in New York in 1995, opening offices in Shanghai and Beijing four years later.

There are enterprising developers with similar ambitions. To date, Zhang Xin and Pan Shiyi have probably made the most impact, with their visionary Soho China lifestyle concept advocating loft-style living. The developer couple also masterminded the Commune-By-The-Wall hotel residences in Beijing, a unique village of eleven country houses individually designed by Asian architects. However, their efforts remain a blip on China's architectural landscape.

The country's appetite for 'international' landmark corporate trophies and cultural symbols continues unabated. It has been argued that the proposed CCTV Headquarters project in Beijing by OMA establishes a different understanding of the boundaries of large-scale commercial typologies. Writing for *Metropolis* magazine (January 2005),

The Beijing National Stadium is the centrepiece of the 2008 Olympic Games. Designed by the Swiss practice Herzog & de Meuron, it is nicknamed 'the bird's nest' because of its mesh-like appearance. The façade and structure are fully integrated as a single gridded entity.

Matt Steinglass explores OMA's rationale, arguing that the trapezoidal loop of woven steel and glass creates something less static than an average skyscraper, whose podium attempts to establish a degree of connectivity to the city. He quotes OMA's Ole Scheeren: "The loop is a non-hierarchical function that connects all the different activities where they can all meet." The line-up for the CCTV competition was a global 'who's who' of celebrity architects. The A-list included SOM, Dominique Perrault, Philip Johnson and KPF, and the international jury comprised stellar names such as Arata Isozaki and Charles Jencks. It is widely acknowledged that OMA invested time and effort to establish a local presence before winning the competition and developing a partnership with the East China Architectural Design & Research Institute. MADA s.p.a.m.'s Qingyun Ma is also involved with the project.

Political correctness can obviously help win friends and influence people, as many foreign architects working in China have discovered. "China is now the largest construction site in the world. That makes us, as architects, excited", Neil Leach, visiting professor at the Dessau Institute of Architecture, announced at a recent seminar on avant-garde architecture at Tsinghua University (quoted in article 'Time for Chinese Architects to Come Out of the "Eggshell"', China Daily, 29 June 2004). Aside from the obvious advantages of cashing in on China's building boom, international practices are also challenged by the opportunity to explore new architectural discourses. Zaha Hadid once described China as "an incredible empty canvas for innovation" (quoted in Time Asia, 3 May 2004). If Mao were alive today, he might remind us of his famous words: "Let a hundred flowers bloom and a hundred schools of thought contend."

According to the Beijing-based Architecture Journal, there are now more than 120 foreign and joint-venture architecture firms with offices in China (China Daily, 29 June 2004). More than 140 of the world's top engineering companies and design consortia have established branches across the country. In both size and speed, the building boom sweeping through China has no precedent. Current statistics reveal that China is investing about $375 billion each year in construction – almost 10% of its gross domestic product. In the process it is using 54.7% of the world's concrete production, 36.1% of its steel and 30.4% of its coal output (Architectural Record, March 2004).

However, overseas architects have not had it easy, and the design and construction process is beset with challenges. Quality is inconsistent, and practices are frequently asked solely to provide conceptual input, leaving the rest to be processed locally. Many have lamented the poor results that are barely recognizable from the original drawings. Conversely, architects may find themselves reworking a project that was half built and then abandoned. The Renaissance Tianjin Teda Hotel and Convention Center was remodelled by Wimberly Allison Tong & Goo from a partially constructed building that had stood untouched for three years. Because of the project's unusual history, principles of feng shui were particularly important in determining the geometry of the adapted structure.

Will the Gold Rush continue, and who has milked the winnings? Not necessarily the architects, but certainly the quest for the newest, boldest and most daring prevails in the knowledge that it is difficult to predict where or when the boom will slow or end, only that it will. Mainstream media enthusiastically report the sky-high budgets allocated to Olympic facilities such as the National Stadium by the Swiss practice Herzog & de Meuron, mammoth infrastructure projects such as the Beijing Capital International Airport by Foster and Partners, and civic landmarks such as the National Grand Theatre of China by Paul Andreu Architecte. Foreign architects working in China have either gone in wholesale on the back of a single project, or have kept at arms' length, operating from a satellite office. Meanwhile, China's own architectural talents are proving that they now have the edge. If there were ever any insecurities over the issue of foreign versus local architectural prowess, this book demonstrates that they have long since dissipated.

CULTURE, LEISURE AND SPORT

BEIJING HOTEL, EAST CHANG'AN AVENUE, BEIJING
NBBJ

**BEIJING TAIWEI JUNLING GOLF CLUB RESORT,
CHANGPING, BEIJING**
INSTITUTE OF ARCHITECTURE DESIGN & RESEARCH,
CHINESE ACADEMY OF SCIENCE

CHINESE MUSEUM OF FILM, BEIJING
RTKL INTERNATIONAL

GUANGDONG MUSEUM, GUANGZHOU
ROCCO DESIGN

GUANGZHOU GYMNASIUM, BAIYUN HILLS, GUANGZHOU
PAUL ANDREU ARCHITECTE

**GUANGZHOU OPERA HOUSE, ZHUJIANG BOULEVARD,
ZHUJIANG NEW TOWN, GUANGZHOU**
ZAHA HADID ARCHITECTS

LOT 107 AND 108, XINTIANDI, SHANGHAI
KOHN PEDERSEN FOX ASSOCIATES

**LUYEYUAN STONE SCULPTURE ART MUSEUM,
XINMIN, CHENGDU**
JIAKUN ARCHITECTS

MUSEUM AND ARCHIVE, PUDONG, SHANGHAI
GMP – VON GERKAN, MARG UND PARTNER ARCHITECTS

NANJING ART AND ARCHITECTURE MUSEUM, NANJING
STEVEN HOLL ARCHITECTS

NATIONAL GRAND THEATRE OF CHINA, BEIJING
PAUL ANDREU ARCHITECTE

NATIONAL MUSEUM OF CHINA, BEIJING
GMP – VON GERKAN, MARG UND PARTNER ARCHITECTS

NINGBO URBAN MUSEUM, NINGBO
MADA S.P.A.M.

OLYMPIC GREEN, BEIJING
SASAKI ASSOCIATES

ORIENTAL ARTS CENTER, SHANGHAI
PAUL ANDREU ARCHITECTE

QINGPU THUMB ISLAND, QINGPU, SHANGHAI
MADA S.P.A.M.

SHANGHAI INTERNATIONAL CIRCUIT, JIADING, SHANGHAI
TILKE ENGINEERS AND ARCHITECTS

SHANGHAI MUSEUM OF SCIENCE & TECHNOLOGY, SHANGHAI
RTKL INTERNATIONAL

SHANGHAI ST REGIS, PUDONG, SHANGHAI
SYDNESS ARCHITECTS

SHENZHEN AQUATIC CENTER, SHENZHEN
COX RICHARDSON ARCHITECTS & PLANNERS

SHENZHEN NO. 2 SENIOR ACTIVITY CENTER, SHENZHEN
OPEN ARCHITECTURE

SHIPAI TOWN HALL, DONGGUAN, GUANGDONG
ATELIER FEICHANG JIANZHU

STADIUM WITH SPORTS PARK, FOSHAN, GUANGDONG
GMP – VON GERKAN, MARG UND PARTNER ARCHITECTS

TIANJIN OLYMPIC CENTER STADIUM, NANKAI, TIANJIN
AXS SATOW

TIANTAI MUSEUM, ZHEJIANG
STUDIO WANG LU IN COLLABORATION WITH ZHEJIANG JIAJING DESIGN
& RESEARCH INSTITUTE

**WATERCUBE NATIONAL SWIMMING CENTER,
BEIJING OLYMPIC GREEN, BEIJING**
PTW ARCHITECTS AND CSCEC-SDI

**WUKESONG CULTURAL AND SPORTS CENTER,
HAI DIAN, BEIJING**
BURCKHARDT+PARTNER

YILANZHAI ART MUSEUM, NANJING
KISHO KUROKAWA ARCHITECT & ASSOCIATES

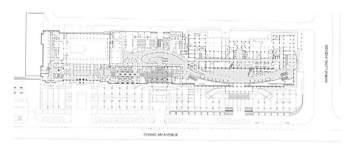

BEIJING HOTEL, EAST CHANG'AN AVENUE, BEIJING

NBBJ, 1999–2002

Prominently positioned on Chang'an Avenue, adjacent to Tiananmen Square, the Beijing Hotel has an illustrious history. Inaugurated nearly a hundred years ago, the hotel has undergone a number of renovations to meet the changing expectations of guests, who include statesmen, business travellers and tourists. While remaining true to its heritage and traditions, it had fallen behind in servicing the technological needs of business guests. Seattle-based NBBJ was commissioned to create a new, identifiable orientation system to link the three hotel buildings, alongside various additions.

The three buildings – the French-style structure, the Chinese-inspired West Building, and the East Building – are connected by a circulation axis that had become weak and diffuse. The curved circulation route stretches over 400 metres, directing guests to the hotel's extensive facilities and casual users to the new entertainment centre.

Built by the French for the diplomatic corps, the original hotel was housed in the Middle Building. NBBJ restored the vaulting and upgraded all the finishes, returning the building to its former glory. The elegant lobby is evocative of a French hotel and is vertically linked into the main axis with

meeting, teleconference, business, banquet and support areas. However, a new Middle Building behind the original is now the hub of the revitalized Beijing Hotel, focused on the grand stair and a dramatic water curtain, which links all four floors and connects them to the French-style building. A dynamic entertainment atrium includes a bowling alley, karaoke rooms and a dance nightspot, while a new health club provides access to the pool.

In the East Building, the primary entrance was upgraded to create a commanding presence on Chang'an Avenue. The linear lobby and winter garden define the major highlights and guide visitors towards the refurbished historic buildings, as well as a new atrium and guest-tower. Restaurants, seating areas and shops overlook the winter garden, which extends the full length of the south façade.

The West Building is also known as the Chinese Building and reflects the nationalism that followed the exile of the Ching emperor. The lobby was remodelled to cater for group business guests and refers thematically to the strictly Chinese Grand Hall. This new lobby employs a similar palette of colours and motifs in a modern spirit.

Opposite
Contemporary features in one of the newly renovated lobby spaces include self-illuminated translucent glass reception desks.

Left
The ground-floor plan and exterior view of the hotel emphasize its three components: the Middle Building, the West Building and the East Building.

The Middle Building forms the dramatic new hub of the hotel.

BEIJING TAIWEI JUNLING GOLF CLUB RESORT, CHANGPING, BEIJING

INSTITUTE OF ARCHITECTURE DESIGN & RESEARCH,
CHINESE ACADEMY OF SCIENCE, 2002–03

Nestled in the valley below the Yanshan Mountains, the Beijing Taiwei Junling Golf Club Resort enjoys a spectacular outlook with a stunning backdrop that offsets its modest composition of forms. The centre is one of a collection of golf clubs and resorts that have flocked to this rural retreat.

At 7065 square metres, the project aims to minimize disturbance to the surrounding natural land forms, its boundaries dictated by the landscape. The architects' intention is to meld architecture with mountains, forests, grassland and sky. The strategic use of ceiling glass brings sky and light into enclosed areas, and every twist and turn is a movement made in deference to the undulating landscape.

The layout is planned so that active spaces progressively give way to quiet, passive functions, creating harmonious comfort for users. With the building spread out along the contours of the topography following the alignment of the mountain, its staggered profile projects a balanced and coherent collage of volumes.

The L-shaped plan of the main structure contains the clubhouse. A central gallery stair provides the main circulation and distributes the principle social spaces, while the changing zone and wet areas make up the furthest portion of the main building. Restaurants, bars and private function rooms are all flexible spaces that can be arranged to suit different gatherings. The major public areas are pushed to the front elevation, where the architectural treatment provides generous window views.

Spanning a floor area of 2810 square metres, the guestrooms occupy a separate block, accessed from the clubhouse via a connecting walkway, which provides greater privacy. On entry, the architecture divides into two wings, whose horizontal planes reach into the landscape like fingers, embracing the natural surroundings.

Above
A concept sketch shows the resort's modest composition of forms in a rural setting.

Below
The building's language is captured through the complex juxtaposition of its forms and the attention paid to connecting features such as the entrance and suspended bridge.

Opposite
The angled arrangement of buildings, along with the site's arching form and discreet entrance, is adapted to the existing site conditions.

CHINESE MUSEUM OF FILM, BEIJING

RTKL INTERNATIONAL, 2002–05

剖面1-1

剖面2-2

Celebrating the achievements of China's movie industry, the Chinese Museum of Film is the country's first facility of its kind. RTKL's scheme, a joint venture with the Beijing Institute of Architectural Design, was selected as the winner of an international competition organized by the Beijing Radio, Film and Television Bureau.

Located in the heart of a planned entertainment district near Beijing's airport, the project is regarded as the centrepiece of a cultural and civic-improvement programme. Its design is therefore expected to contribute considerable visual drama. The Chinese Museum of Film totals 30,000 square metres, including four exhibition halls allotted to film history, film technology and temporary exhibitions; a cinema complex with an IMAX theatre, a 3D theatre, a small review hall and a multifunctional hall; collection and storage, research and administrative offices.

Working alongside the China Film Museum Project Committee, RTKL developed a design that applies a synthetic approach, taking direct inspiration from and elevating the popular art of film. The building evolved by restructuring a mixture of the basic characteristics and visual tropes of cinema and architecture. Taking their cue from a universal cinema icon – the production clapperboard – giant translucent glass walls covered in projected images are angled towards the main public access areas. These walls create angles of intersection that evoke the motion of the closing clapperboard.

The design of the museum lays particular emphasis not only on the rich history of film throughout China, but also on an architectural language that is sensitive to design languages that closely represent local experiences, maximizing self-sustained integrity while at the same time encouraging flexibility and environmental responsibility. Chinese gardens, which are celebrated for their controlled vistas and as spaces for improvisational views, are reinterpreted to serve as theatres for showcasing films.

Opposite
The museum includes four exhibition halls for film history, film technology and temporary exhibits. Large screens provide dynamic projections of Chinese films throughout the museum.

Above
The angles of the museum's façade take their cue from the production clapperboard, that universally recognized symbol of cinema.

Sections through long and end elevations reveal the museum's major internal functions.

GUANGDONG MUSEUM, GUANGZHOU

ROCCO DESIGN, 2004–06

This proposal for a new museum of arts and history won an invited international competition. The commission envisages the creation of a stunning civic landmark at the confluence of Guangzhou's new city centre, Zhujiang, and the Pearl River Delta. The building will form part of a Cultural and Art Square development (including an opera house by Zaha Hadid) that plugs into the main city axis, melting into a fluid landscape towards the banks of the river.

The 4.1-hectare site is expected to accommodate 60,000 square metres in floor area, around a third of which will be below ground. Four main exhibition halls allow flexibility for temporary exhibitions. Additional facilities for research, administration and visitor services are also incorporated. The museum is understood as a precious object, holding the key to priceless works of art and historic materials. It is conceived as both a container protecting these valuables and as a treasure box in itself. The idea is developed from traditional highly decorated Chinese lacquered caskets and the intricate lace-like carvings of multilayered ivory balls.

The treasure chest is enveloped in a formidable casing of ash-grey metallic cladding. The smooth geometric linear box is chiselled with numerous patterns that appear randomly across the façades. These openings allow glimpses through to the layers within; for visitors inside they are windows to the views outside. The form appears to be raised from the ground owing to the unbroken landscape that flows beneath it. Uncluttered by other structures, it permits users fully to contemplate the museum's presence.

Internally, the spaces are organized in concentric layers, so visitors are invited to penetrate deeper and deeper before finally reaching the central core. This innermost void is a dramatic counterpoint to the outer spaces, a pristine courtyard that distils the southern Chinese theme in its exhibits and forms the most intense expression of the museum's identity.

Besides creating an intriguing journey through the building, the layering principle addresses the need for clear functional zoning and circulation. Pathways of different sizes link the exhibition halls, providing easy access to the exhibits however they are configured. The carved walls partially reveal the activities taking place further in, arousing curiosity while fixing orientation. Breathing spaces between the larger halls are more intimate in scale, with an intricate geometry that filters natural light and encourages visitors to pause before continuing.

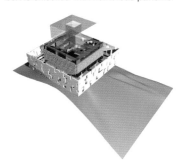

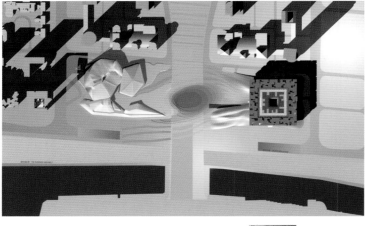

Left and above
In plan and form the museum building resembles a precious, intricately carved Chinese casket.

Opposite
An intriguing journey awaits visitors as they begin to explore the museum spaces.

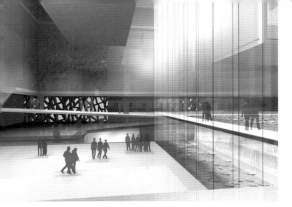

GUANGZHOU GYMNASIUM, BAIYUN HILLS, GUANGZHOU

PAUL ANDREU ARCHITECTE, 1998–2001

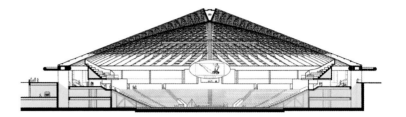

Built in time to host the closing ceremony of the Ninth National Games in 2001, the Guangzhou Gymnasium joins a plethora of well-equipped sports venues around the city. Situated at the foot of the Baiyun Hills near the old airport on the fringe of the city, the area forms part of a protected landscape in an 18-hectare park where building is not permitted. Paul Andreu has attempted to create a smooth transition between city and countryside with the intention of preserving the views of the natural landscape.

The special qualities of the site called for a low-lying structure inflicting minimal impact on its surroundings. The architect extended the concept by breaking up the building into three components, reducing its mass and enhancing its humanly scaled proportions. The requirements of the programme are met by burying some activities underground; this produces enough space to accommodate major sporting events.

Visually, the architecture emerges from the earth as three shell-like structures with protruding semi-transparent roof elements. The buildings themselves can be read as geometrically pure 'hills', evolving their own microlandscape within the broader natural environment. Each building hosts a primary function: the main stadium, the training hall and a public sports centre. A ceremonial area is intentionally orientated outside the buildings so that participants can enjoy views across the valley.

The translucent roof forms are constructed on a concrete base with a lightweight steel structure clad in semi-transparent panels. Within the sports facilities, the glare of sunlight is filtered by the roof to produce very uniform, evenly balanced illumination that is perfect for viewing events and broadcasting. Unlike the hugely muscular structures that are typically designed as stadia, these modest and distinctive entities blend comfortably with the landscape.

Above
A section through the main stadium reveals the space created to accommodate some activities underground.

Semi-transparent roof panels filter out the glare of natural light.

Opposite
The shell-like buildings fit comfortably into the rolling landscape while creating the large volumes needed to host major sporting events.

1 - Main Hall
2 - Training Hall
3 - Mass Sport Center
4 - Athletes Village
5 - Administration Building
6 - Parking
7 - Restaurant
8 - Garden

GUANGZHOU OPERA HOUSE, ZHUJIANG BOULEVARD, ZHUJIANG NEW TOWN, GUANGZHOU

ZAHA HADID ARCHITECTS, 2003–07

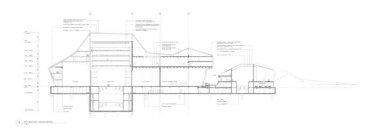

Sited close to the busy Pearl River, Guangzhou Opera House has an unusual profile, the fluid contours of the two buildings representing the higher notes of the Chinese opera and the tenor pitch of its Western sibling. This 'global family' gathered together is regarded by the architect as a testament to the state of art architecture and a lasting monument to the new millennium. The buildings also provide open access to the riverbanks and dock areas and create a new dialogue with the emerging new town.

The evolution of this project, for the Guangzhou municipal government, began with a landscape of undulating structures that rise and fall from the foot of Zhujiang Boulevard. New structures tie together the two adjacent opera house buildings as well as future museum sites and metropolitan activities.

The terraced profile of the dual sites presents a riverfront focus to visitors and provides an adjunct to the Haixinsha Tourist Park Island. Likewise, from the perspective of the park, the opera house creates a

visual prelude to the Tourist Park Island. It negotiates a difficult position between the waterfront and the modern commercial towers of Zhujiang New Town. In response, the architect has tried hard to create a unified vision of the civic and cultural buildings in this emerging riverside setting.

The programme for the 46,000-square-metre project comprises a 1800-seat grand theatre, entrance lobby and lounge, multifunction hall and support facilities. An internal street is carved into the landforms from the opposite side of the landscaped central boulevard, where the new museum is planned. The more public facilities, such as the café, bar, restaurant and shops, are embedded into the landforms and located along one edge of the promenade leading to the opera house. Visitors arriving by car or bus are deposited at a drop-off point on the north side of the site on Huajiu Road. Service vehicles access the opera house and theatre buildings at either end of the Huajiu Road, while VIPs enter from the western boundary facing Huaxia Road.

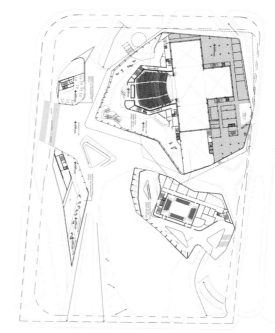

Right
A section and site plan illustrate how the two buildings of the opera house fit closely together.

The striking interior of the 1800-seat grand theatre.

Opposite
Renderings of the opera house show the two structures embedded in the contoured landscape in relation to the main axis of Zhujiang New Town.

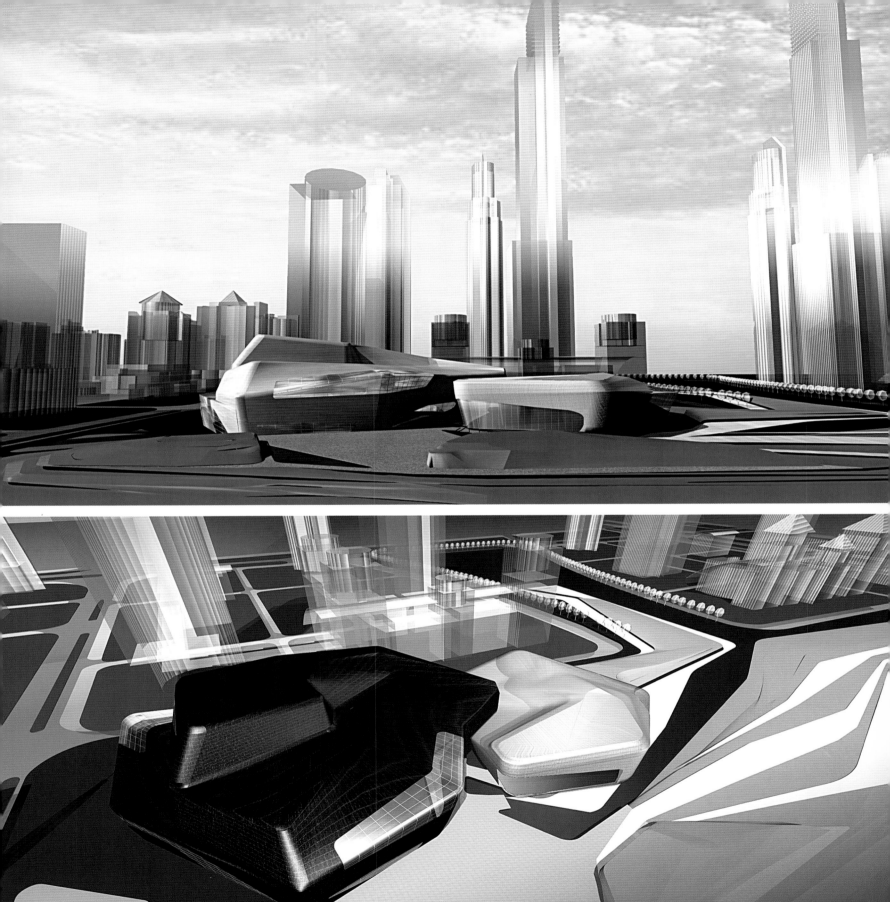

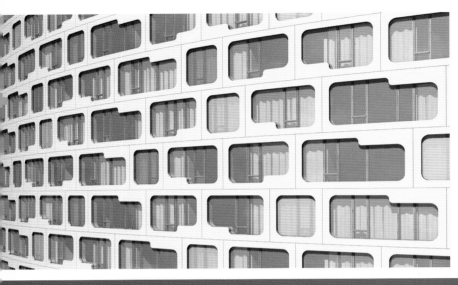

LOT 107 AND 108, XINTIANDI, SHANGHAI

KOHN PEDERSEN FOX ASSOCIATES, 2003–07

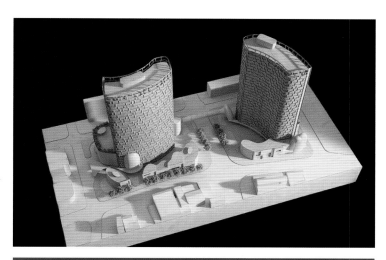

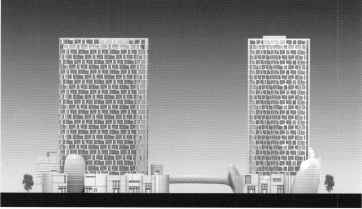

The restored *shikumen* houses at Xintiandi – now magnets for shopping, dining and entertainment – are getting new neighbours in the form of two luxury hotel developments. The 86,500-square-metre project comprises two blocks within their own grounds set back from the low-rise enclave. Besides guest accommodation, the five-star properties will include facilities such as a grand ballroom, business and meeting facilities, spa and retail areas.

Owing to their large scale, the articulation and orientation of the simple curvilinear towers have created a major challenge for the architects and the owner, Shanghai Li Xing Hotels. Although mirrored in form, the crescent-like blocks bulge in different directions, avoiding the negative connotations of a rear elevation. The potential harshness of the forms is also reduced by smoothing off the corners of the buildings.

However, the most striking aspect of the buildings is the intricate façade that forms a continuous veil around each tower. The window pattern varies subtly between the two structures: that for Lot 108 is derived from a traditional Chinese lattice-work design, while Lot 107's is a modern and playful twist on the same motif. Using a light-coloured stone, the 'screen' continues beyond the top of the building so that at night the tips will radiate a soft glow through the unglazed openings.

Functionally, the major hotel spaces are contained within a 24-metre-high podium that fills the north-east side of Lot 107 and the north-west side of Lot 108. At the south-west corner of Lot 107 a bar and jazz club are featured in a glazed sculptural form that highlights the activity inside. Retail occupies a two-and-a half-storey venue on the southern edge of the sites. The relatively modest scale here meets the similarly proportioned structures across the street. The stone cladding along this edge also helps to retain the intimate pedestrian character of Tai Cang Lu.

Opposite
The lattice-work façade of the two towers is offset by the sculptural, glassy entertainment venue.

Above
An aerial view of the model and an exterior rendering highlight the relationship between the two buildings and their surroundings.

LUYEYUAN STONE SCULPTURE ART MUSEUM, XINMIN, CHENGDU

JIAKUN ARCHITECTS, 2001–02

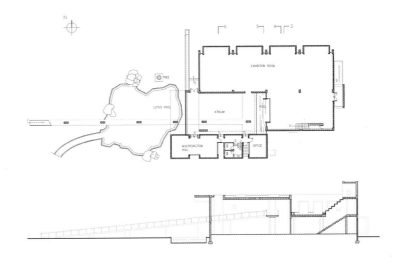

Located in the village of Yunqiao on a site that was initially a 6670-square-metre field straddling a river and a stretch of woodland, the museum is made up of four major components. The largest zone, totalling 990 square metres, is reserved for the principal exhibition spaces, while the rest of the space is taken up by carparks, an open exhibition area and a subsidiary building. Bamboo groves form natural divisions between these entities. The different parts of the project are strung together by natural bamboo-lined walkways before visitors reach the entrance that bridges over a lotus pond.

The museum installations are laid out around an atrium where the architecture creates an interplay between the light, the exhibits and the landscape. The organization owes much to the architects' careful handling of the gaps between the various building blocks.

Addressing the content of the museum collections – stone sculptures – the architecture seeks a dialogue by narrating a story of 'artificial stone'. Relying on local construction techniques, which are limited yet flexible enough to allow subsequent modification, the architecture is predominantly defined by a frame structure of fair-faced concrete and shale bricks.

The bricks on the inner face of the layered walls are used as a template to ensure the concrete is poured vertically, but also to facilitate later modifications as a soft lining. Striated indentation templates receive the poured concrete to form the walls of the main building, creating a clear pattern and a strong, monolithic impression. Any potential defects resulting from poor pouring techniques are masked by the richly textured lattice of the façade.

Above
A plan and section emphasize the layering of walls and spaces.

Below
The exhibition and circulation areas are characterized by controlled light and neutral surfaces.

Opposite
The museum is built along the edge of a river, and visitors reach its entrance by a bridge over a lotus pond.

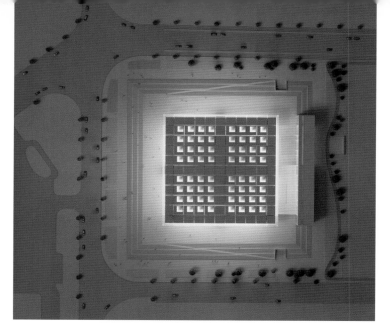

MUSEUM AND ARCHIVE, PUDONG, SHANGHAI

GMP – VON GERKAN, MARG UND PARTNER ARCHITECTS, 2002–05

Located among the new glassy towers of the business district of Pudong, across the Huangpu River from the historic Bund, the Museum and Archive is a museum and exhibition hall that will trace the origins of Pudong and its meteoric rise, documenting and archiving the evidence of the area's evolution into Shanghai's financial and business hub.

The project results from an international competition held in 2002, in which Meinhard von Gerkan was awarded first prize. Working alongside the Shanghai Institute of Architectural Design & Research, the architect has designed modern, multifunctional and open exhibition spaces totalling 41,000 square metres in gross floor area.

One of the principal architectural features of the museum is its pedestal, which lifts the main building and exhibition halls above street level, emphasizing the complex's significance. Simplicity and a limited palette of materials define the characteristics of the clear cube, whose diagram conforms to a square floor layout.

The composition assembles three major elements: the square-shaped main building, which contains the museum's central functions; a wider 4-metre-high pedestal with stairs around it, which accommodates the archives; and a bar-shaped building on the eastern side for administration.

The façade of the upper, closed part of the main building serves a dual purpose as weather protection and as a medium of communication to passers-by. It is composed of two parallel layers, the outer made of glass and the inner comprising solid wall panels. The panels can be rotated along their longitudinal axis, allowing them to be opened and closed according to different exhibition needs. Open, they let visitors catch views of the surrounding urban fabric while giving people outside a taste of what lies within.

The transparent glass skin conveys the content of the archive in tiny patterned forms, which create a bigger picture when seen from a distance. In exposed areas movies or graphics can be projected on to the semi-transparent glass by projectors mounted in wall recesses.

Opposite

The distinctive horizontal form of the exterior contrasts with its vertical urban surroundings.

The inner spaces are designed as flexible exhibition halls with rotating panels.

Left

An aerial view highlights the perforated roof of the complex.

The complex's crystalline glass skin acts as a communication medium.

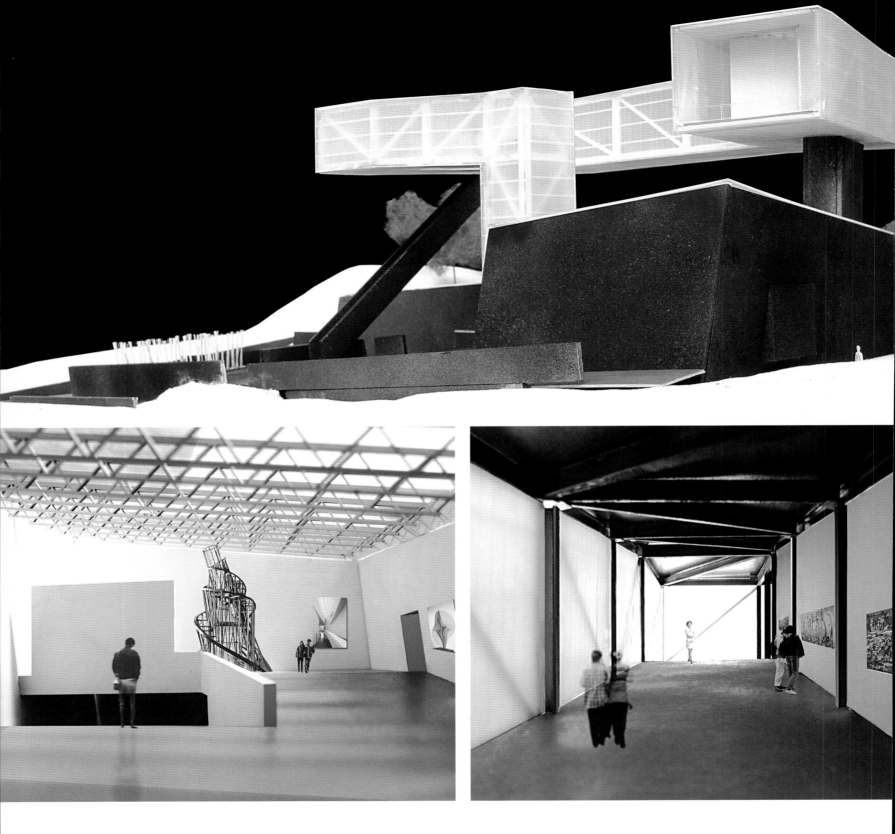

NANJING ART AND ARCHITECTURE MUSEUM, NANJING

STEVEN HOLL ARCHITECTS, 2003–06

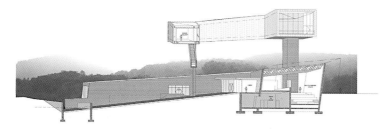

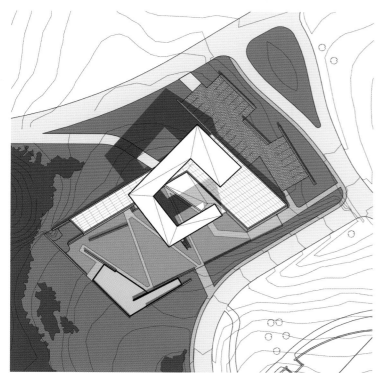

This new museum forms a gateway to the CIPEA (China Practical Exhibition of Architecture) exhibition area in the lush, green landscape of the Pearl Spring near Nanjing. The work of twenty international architects, curated by Arata Isozaki, will be the first exhibition to be hosted in the venue.

The project began in an exploration of the 'parallel perspectives' of Chinese art. The fundamental historical difference between Western and Chinese painting lies in the treatment of perspective. From the thirteenth century on, Western paintings adopted vanishing points in fixed perspective. Chinese painters rejected this method in favour of producing landscapes with parallel perspectives, where the viewer travels within the painting. Shifting viewpoints, layers of space, expanses of mist and water all characterize the deep, alternating spatial mysteries that compose Chinese paintings.

With this in mind, the museum is conceived as a 'field' of parallel perspective spaces and garden walls constructed of black rammed earth, over which a translucent constructed 'figure' hovers. The linear passages at ground level gradually transform into the winding route of the figure above, which culminates in a view of the city of Nanjing in the distance. The section of the figure, with its translucent walls and floor, is an inversion of the section of the building, with its translucent ceiling, below. The ceiling is constructed from a framework of solar collectors, which permit 30% of natural light to penetrate the interior.

Designed in association with the Architectural Design Institute at Nanjing University, the 3000-square-metre museum contains flexible exhibition spaces, a teahouse and the curator's residence. These facilities face the southern light and recirculated water of the pond. The 'green' aims of the project are embodied in the geothermal cooling and heating system, recycled materials and low-embodied-energy materials.

Opposite
Perspectives highlight the dual nature of the museum structure.

The internal exhibition spaces are fed with controlled natural light.

Left
A section, plan and model emphasize the linear circulation of the museum and its progressive transformation into an intricate, meandering route.

NATIONAL GRAND THEATRE OF CHINA, BEIJING

PAUL ANDREU ARCHITECTE, 1999–2005

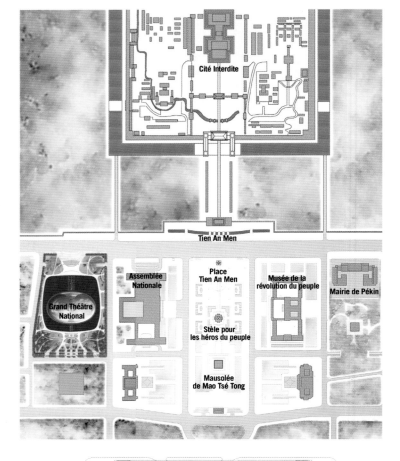

Situated in the heart of Beijing's historic centre, adjacent to the Great Hall of the People and a stone's throw from Tiananmen Square, the National Grand Theatre is conceived as a cultural island in the middle of a lake. The building, designed by French architect Paul Andreu, takes the form of a gently curving dome, whose titanium-clad façade is peeled back from the glazed wall like the leading edge of a parting curtain.

The 46-metre-high 'super-ellipsoid' structure has a total surface area of 149,500 square metres and spans that reach as wide as 144 metres. Completely surrounded by water with no visible means of access, its uninterrupted reflection in the lake creates an aura of mystery. Curving glass stretches up to the roof, allowing daylight to penetrate the inner spaces. At night the interiors become a spectacle to those outside as the building is lit up.

Entry is via a 60-metre-long transparent underpass; visitors feel that they are leaving their daily lives behind as they are introduced to another world. There are three performance auditoriums: a 2416-seat opera house, a 2017-seat concert hall and

a 1040-seat theatre – as well as art and exhibition spaces. A lounge at the top level provides unprecedented perspectives across the city for both theatre-goers and the general public.

Public spaces within the building have been developed as an 'urban district' with streets, plazas, shopping areas, restaurants, relaxation lounges and meeting areas. The aim is to create an environment that is open and appealing to the widest-possible audience rather than restricted and elitist. The primary circulation links directly into the performance spaces with the opera house placed at the very centre. The last is regarded as not only the most significant component of the project, but also the most traditional and mysterious. Its symbolic nature is conveyed by a distinctive architecture covered in gilt-metal mesh, a shell that becomes partially transparent when illuminated.

The architect has tried to create a building that respects the historic and cultural richness of its neighbours, and also celebrates the vitality of modern architecture head-on.

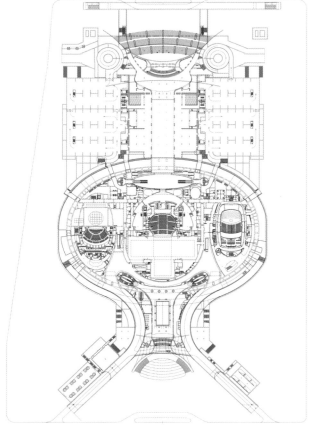

Right
Visitors access the theatre building via a long transparent underpass – shown on the masterplan and plan – that crosses the lake.

Opposite
The 'super ellipsoid' is clad in curved glass, allowing daylight to penetrate the inner spaces.

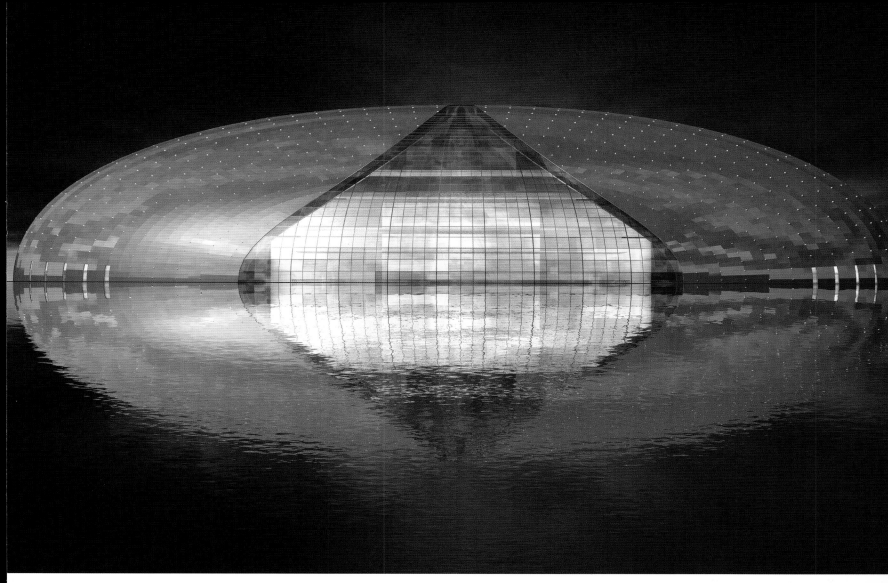

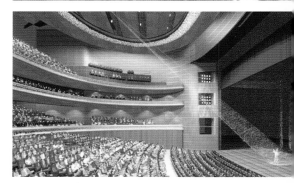

NATIONAL MUSEUM OF CHINA, BEIJING

GMP – VON GERKAN, MARG UND PARTNER ARCHITECTS, 2004–07

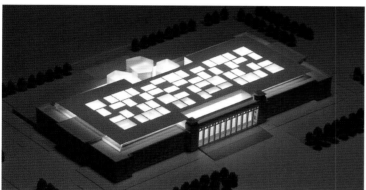

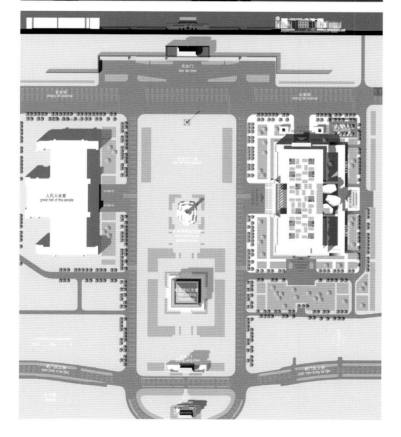

Located on the eastern side of Tiananmen Square, the museum serves as an extension to the Great Hall of the People. In its current state, the museum is lent dignity by its high colonnades, but inside it lacks openness and transparency, being obstructed by a central entrance building. The entrance separates the two U-shaped wings of the museum – the Chinese History Museum and the Revolutionary Museum. When the programmes of the two museums are unified under the umbrella of the National Museum of China, this central circulation point will be functionless. The architects' proposal, which won first prize in an international competition in 2004, removes this entrance, generating a spacious foyer while connecting both entrances from the north and west sides.

The museum's new image is encapsulated by its roof form, which covers an open public space and provides shelter from sun and rain. Its eaves rise to 34.5 metres in order to create a balance in terms of scale and proportion with the Great Hall of the People. However, its slender silhouette avoids expressive and sensational architectural gestures. The intention is to focus on improving the quality of space in relation to Tiananmen Square and to establish a dialogue between the two civic buildings. Nevertheless, the roof will form a dynamic symbol, clad in bronze panels in acknowledgement of the museum's most highly treasured works of art. The material will have a matt golden finish on its underside where it is visible from Tiananmen Square, establishing a clear relationship with the parapet of the existing building as well as with other structures around the square.

With a generous 170,000 square metres of space, China's national museum will be one of the largest institutions of its kind anywhere. Responding to the high volume of traffic expected to pass through its doors, the grand forum is essentially an extension of the urban public space. Its outer envelope – walls, ceilings and so on – all help to orientate visitors towards the various exhibition spaces, including the general- and special-display areas located in the roof volume. The planning aims to provide multiple ways to access the collections. In the spirit of traditional Chinese architecture, ramps, stairs and podiums intersect in the forum, creating layers of viewpoints. The monumental red cores and the cantilevered roof also provide local cultural and architectural references.

Opposite
The grand forum orientates the museum's exhibition spaces via ramps, stairs and terraces. Even its roof volume accommodates general and special displays.

Left
The underside of the museum's iconic roof is visible from Tiananmen Square, and at night it radiates a subtle glow.

The site plan shows the museum in relation to the square and the major buildings around it.

NINGBO URBAN MUSEUM, NINGBO

MADA S.P.A.M., 2002–03

This project involved the conversion of an old warehouse next to a dock. The intervention breathes new life into an abandoned structure through minimal and economical architectural means. Recognizing that the city of Ningbo has a special history and anticipating a successful future, MADA s.p.a.m. wanted to acknowledge the cultural heritage as well as the community's entrepreneurial spirit in the museum project. Taking the view that the city is an accumulation of productive human mechanisms, lifestyles and faiths, a composite of multiple layers and multiple dimensions emerged.

The warehouse building is generous in height and width, making it flexible, but also simple and logical in its structure. While making use of the large generic floorplates that characterize the building, the architects overlay a circulation trajectory in order to maximize the amount of exhibition space.

This gesture is expressed on the façade, which is treated simply as a translucent wrapper made from glass block throughout, a traditional material that is now considered unfashionable. The façade's subtle colour changes are achieved by applying different paints to the sides of the blocks before they are sealed in the factory.

Conceptually, the project combines three strategies. First, the aim is to put the exhibits into the context of the region's current culture. Secondly, the museum is regarded as the point at which the city's various urban characteristics converge. Thirdly, the architects want the museum to be understood as a microcosm of Ningbo. The museum accommodates internal and external exhibition areas, a forum for visitor discussions, a leisure centre with café, restaurant, bookshop and other retail uses, offices, production and storage spaces.

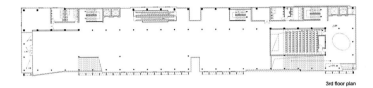

3rd floor plan

2nd floor plan

1st floor plan

Right
Plans and a long section of the three-storey building reveal its simple and logical structure.

Opposite
The view from the city waterfront shows the museum's dockyard location.

The intricately articulated façade subtly displays the architectural insertions.

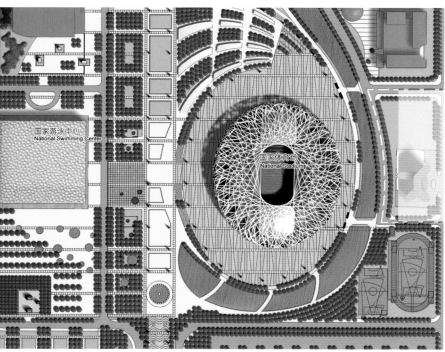

Above
An aerial perspective of Olympic Green looks towards the National Stadium from the canal eco-zone.

Left
A magnified plan details the National Stadium and Swimming Center Plaza.

Opposite
Site plans show the central axis and landscape proposal for the core area.

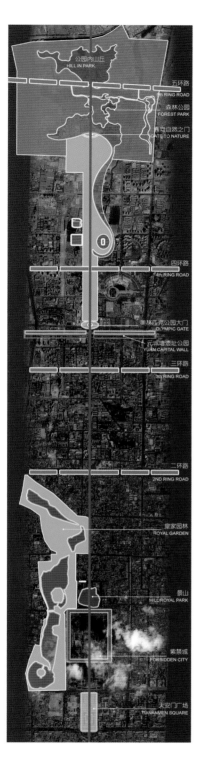

OLYMPIC GREEN, BEIJING

SASAKI ASSOCIATES, 2002–08

Sasaki Associates' award-winning masterplan for the Olympic Green – the main competition venue of the 2008 Summer Olympic Games in Beijing – was the result of an international design competition. The Olympic Green is both an ambitious, unprecedented effort at city building and an opportunity to host the 29th Olympiad in a setting of immense historical and cultural richness.

Sasaki's scheme was supported by the Tianjin Architecture Institute. It seeks balance and integration in both poetic and pragmatic terms, establishing a connection to the environmental ideal rooted in the myths and legends of ancient China, while being firmly grounded in the twenty-first century in its recognition of the fundamentals of sustainability.

Subsequently, a further competition was held to establish the site's landscape design. Sasaki, working in collaboration with the Tsinghua Planning Institute, was again selected as the winner.

Three fundamental elements make up Sasaki's concept, which seeks to express the modern Olympic ideals of sport, culture and environment. There is the Forest Park and its extension southwards; the Cultural Axis extending north to conclude in the great eight-hundred-year-old imperial axis; and the Olympic Axis, which links the Asian Games site with the National Stadium, ultimately intersecting with the Cultural Axis.

The Forest Park is conceived as the ideal paradise from which Chinese civilization emerged many millennia ago. Sculptural hills, forests and meadows are built up by excavating the ground to create the Dragon Lake. They gradually give way to more formal open space, as water from the lake flows south into a canal adjoining the esplanade. This is arranged like a dragon's tail, symbolically linking the major components of the plan through nature.

The Cultural Axis makes use of the north–south axis on which Beijing was founded, extending it some 5 km through the Olympic Green site. The scale is monumental, emphasizing its significance in order to balance the powerful simplicity of the Forest Park at the opposite end.

The Olympic Axis begins with the existing Asian Games Stadium, extending north-east to encompass the proposed National Stadium and continuing into a Sports Heroes Garden, which then intersects with the Cultural Axis, concluding with an Olympic Spirit Park within the Forest Park. Where the Olympic Axis meets the Cultural Axis, Sasaki has created Zhou Dynasty Plaza, commemorating China's contributions to city building.

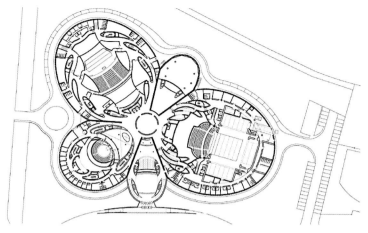

ORIENTAL ARTS CENTER, SHANGHAI

PAUL ANDREU ARCHITECTE, 2000–04

Located on Century Avenue in Shanghai's new Pudong district, the Oriental Arts Center is one of the city's most important cultural venues. Designed by French architect Paul Andreu, the project encompasses three main arenas: a 1979-seat philharmonic orchestra hall, a 1054-seat lyric theatre and a 330-seat chamber-music hall. Other amenities include an exhibition hall, music retailers, a restaurant and an arts resource and training facility.

The 4-hectare site is constructed on seven levels. The architect conceived what he describes as a 'familiar object' in the heart of the city, existing purely to add to the beauty of the urban fabric and for the pleasure of residents and visitors. The sculptural pearl-grey form does not instantly reveal its functional nature; furthermore, the building transforms itself gradually as one goes round it. Its scalloped structures widen out as they reach for the sky, unified and sheltered by a single cantilevered roof.

A flight of steps ascends to the entrance opposite the town hall. The transparency is most apparent here, with a further staircase and vivid accents of colour inviting exploration. The other glass façades incorporate perforated metal sheets of varying density; through them, the light-filled spaces present a glowing, coloured lantern to the community at night.

Performance halls and public spaces emerge from the base of the three volumes, creating a central circulation and meeting point for theatre-goers, performers and public. While the three venues are each distinctive in form and material, they all feature enamelled ceramic wrapping their outer walls. The intertwined circulation zones around them are clearly legible and identified by curves and transparency. Rooted in the solid base are spaces for artists and production teams to prepare for their shows. Rehearsal and dressing rooms line the periphery, supported by a central lounge and technical facility. The atmosphere is calm and serene in order to foster focus, concentration and thought.

Opposite
The major performance halls and theatres evolve from three sculpted building forms.

Left
The plan outlines the distinctive forms of the three venues.

An intertwined circulation system guides visitors from the formal entrance to the grand interiors of the performance halls.

QINGPU THUMB ISLAND, QINGPU, SHANGHAI

MADA S.P.A.M., 2003–05

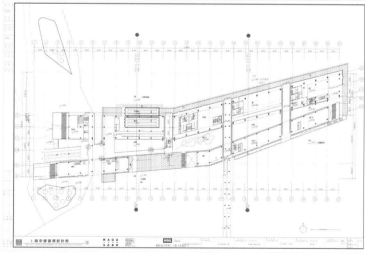

Located on a man-made lake on the outskirts of Shanghai's metropolitan area, the Qingpu Thumb Island project is a new cultural institution that will serve the rapidly expanding population of the place. Together with other recently proposed buildings with various functions, the project is seen as defining a new civic centre for Qingpu, a metropolis that is experiencing rapid growth.

The architecture is perceived as an extension of the landscape edge of the lake, forming a thumb-like green peninsula. Deeply inscribed, the structure unfurls into the body of the water, harking back to the philosophy of Chinese landscape – the interplay of space, materials and energy set in a continuous flux between the man-made and the natural.

Qingpu Thumb Island integrates the Chinese philosophy of views, amusement and habitation in landscape design, simultaneously engaging users with the building and the water's edge. A flowing green band rises and undulates across the site, providing a focal point in the middle of the lake. The same logic is continued inside, penetrating all the programmatic functions at various elevations. The architects compare the building to a giant piece of rock, whose mass is riddled with grottoes and channels forming intimate spatial relationships.

In order to control the way sunlight is admitted to the building, materials with different degrees of transparency are applied to the façade. These provide subtle variations in the experience for visitors as their journeys unravel. Users are able to choose both their destinations and the paths they take to reach them, including the route to the pinnacle of the rock, where trees and planting compose a partial view of the lake.

Opposite
Views of the model and detail renderings highlight the interaction of pedestrians with the building and the water.

Left
The masterplan, ground-floor plan and a section show the undulating structure unfurling into the man-made lake.

SHANGHAI INTERNATIONAL CIRCUIT, JIADING, SHANGHAI

TILKE ENGINEERS AND ARCHITECTS, 2002–04

Covering an area of 146 hectares, the Shanghai International Circuit is a Formula One racetrack designed by Tilke in co-operation with the Shanghai Institute of Architectural Design & Research. The facility incorporates the latest race-circuit technology and strikes an appropriate image for the twenty-first century.

The architects referred to the Chinese character 'Shang', meaning 'high' or 'above', in devising the composition of the new racetrack. Expressing modernity as well as recalling China's history, the architecture makes cultural references through colours, materials and forms, combined with the high technology of Formula One racing.

The red and gold chosen for the roof of the main grandstand are auspicious Chinese colours, representing fortune and power. The PTFE-membrane roofs of the two opposing grandstands to the south-east of the track are constructed in the form of lotus leaves.

The twenty-six team buildings behind the pit building are arranged like pavilions on a lake. They are modelled on the famed Yu Yuan Garden in Shanghai and inject a note of tranquility into the hubbub and noise of a motor-sport event. For flexibility, each building can be converted into two hotel rooms.

The media centre and restaurant hover like wings over the track, extending almost 140 metres in length. The materials used – aluminium, glass and stainless steel – reflect the speed and high-technology of Formula One and its home. The rear elevations of the grandstands, which can hold up to 200,000 spectators, form an imposing entrance. They are faced with stainless-steel mesh that is permeable to light and air. Its texture changes during the course of the day, veering between shiny metallic or transparent in response to the varying daylight. At night it is self-illuminated, creating a dramatic glow.

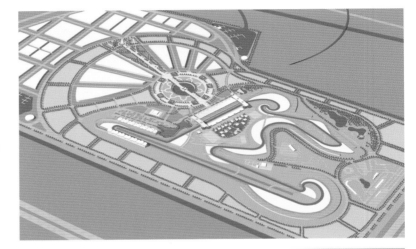

Right
Site plan and distant view of the circuit buildings in relation to the racetrack.

Opposite
Juxtaposition of the opposing spectator stands against their contrasting roof forms – the free-form membrane structures and the lens-shaped media centre and restaurant.

SHANGHAI MUSEUM OF SCIENCE & TECHNOLOGY, SHANGHAI

RTKL INTERNATIONAL, 1998–2001

The commission for the Shanghai Scienceland Development Company's new science and technology centre was awarded to RKTL after an international competition. The architects were faced with the challenge of embracing the past in a culturally sensitive manner while representing the future of a rapidly emerging high-tech city. The result is an architectural statement that is conceived as a civic and educational icon for both residents and visitors.

The 89,000-square-metre project is an educational institute for the new millennium, designed to promote advances in science and technology. Located along the southern edge of Civic Plaza, opposite a prominent government building and near Central Park, the museum complex comprises two buildings. The four-storey main building houses five galleries themed under the titles Universe, Living, Intelligence, Innovation and Future. Visitors can enter the galleries at any point.

RTKL's asymmetrical design curves around Civic Plaza and establishes a strong axis through the complex. The building is divided between a tall, airy exhibit space on one side and enclosed auditoriums on the other. Translucent and reflective glass is used extensively. The façade overlooking Civic Plaza is essentially transparent, bringing the activity there seamlessly inside and creating an impression of fluid movement through the building. The entrance hub is a large elliptical ball, which, combined with a decorative hanging sphere, takes the form of an egg and its yolk, an important Chinese symbol.

Expressing the harmony between man and nature, the five essential elements of Chinese culture – metal, wood, water, fire and earth – are symbolically represented in the design of the building and its landscaping. Indigenous stone complements metal wall panels and introduces natural elements into the structure. Other traditional materials are used in concert with modern, sustainable materials to show the relationship between past and future, science and man.

Top
The roof of the museum is designed to represent the unlimited potential of man and science.

Above and left
Atrium, roof and entrance details highlight the extensive use of glass.

Opposite
The entrance hub and the façade of the museum curve around Civic Plaza.

SHANGHAI ST REGIS, PUDONG, SHANGHAI

SYDNESS ARCHITECTS, 1998–2001

This international five-star hotel occupies a prominent site in the heart of Shanghai's new business enclave in Pudong. Rising forty storeys and clad in red Chinese granite, the building's distinctive slender profile is expressed in a grid format that corresponds to the hotel's guestroom module and storey height. At almost 45 square metres, the hotel's 318 guestrooms are the largest Shanghai has to offer. The tower culminates in two gently curving peaks that are set at different heights and point in opposite directions, making the most of the breathtaking views from the two stylish restaurants that occupy the top floors.

A 23-metre-high podium structure contains the hotel's central functions, including the four-storey lobby, the ballroom, three dining venues, a fitness centre and business/conference facilities. The swimming pool is an exception, located on the fifth floor with a skylit ceiling and open views to the south.

Inspired by the grand opera houses of an earlier era, the interiors have richly coloured finishes, textured fabrics and elegant furnishings. Asian art and antique furniture add regional touches to the otherwise contemporary palette, while voluminous draperies create a sense of theatre. Natural elements are provided by groves of bamboo in shallow reflective pools that create the meditative sounds of trickling water.

Guests enter the 650-square-metre lobby under a stunning bronze-framed glass enclosure to be greeted by a soaring space featuring a grand, sweeping stair. This connects the lobby to the mezzanine lounge before continuing up to reach the ballroom and pre-function areas. The mezzanine gallery provides a captivating vantage point overlooking the lobby below, its elliptical form echoing the soft arcs of the tower's architecture and the overall plan of the hotel. The theme is accentuated by inlaid marble floors and crimson marble columns that give order to the space; its crowning glory is a glowing onyx ovoid ceiling feature.

Ground Floor Plan

Right
The ground-floor plan indicates the orientation of the entrance and lobby.

The softly curving peaks of the forty-storey tower generate a distinctive profile.

Opposite
The main lobby with its lofty ceilings and sweeping staircase links with the lobby bar.

Each of the dining facilities is distinctively styled.

SHENZHEN AQUATIC CENTER, SHENZHEN
COX RICHARDSON ARCHITECTS & PLANNERS, 1999–2002

Built for the Eleventh Games of Guangdong Province in 2002, the 50,000-square-metre Shenzhen Aquatic Center is one of the most advanced facilities of its type anywhere in the world. Cox Richardson was selected following an international design competition for the swimming and diving halls organized by the Shenzhen Sports Development Institute in December 1999.

Like most of today's advanced sporting venues, usage is not restricted to top-league competitors. The client wanted a watersports complex that would serve both elite athletes and the Shenzhen community. Revenue has to be maximized, and this means encouraging access by the whole local community.

The programme incorporated swimming and diving halls with associated technical and training facilities. Spectator seating is integrated with public amenities such as the restaurant. An indoor leisure park includes pools and dry sports among other attractions, while outdoor pools are connected to landscaped gardens and a waterslide. Access to the centre is defined by a ceremonial plaza; a secondary public entrance has above- and underground parking.

Innovative engineering techniques were required to build the structure's physical form and to achieve its environmental goals. Perhaps the most striking feature of the building is the steel-cable-stayed roof spanning 115 × 70 metres, comparable to the largest of its type anywhere in the world. The building's architecture is also a model of sustainability. The facility is designed to minimize energy use wherever possible by providing natural ventilation and cooling to spectators rather than constant artificial air-conditioning.

Opposite and top left
The steel-cable-stayed roof – one of the largest structures of this type anywhere in the world – and glass-encased stairwells are two of the most striking features of the building.

Left
Beneath the curved roof, the diving pool offers world-class facilities that are virtually unparalleled anywhere else worldwide.

SHENZHEN NO. 2 SENIOR ACTIVITY CENTER, SHENZHEN

OPEN ARCHITECTURE, 2003–06

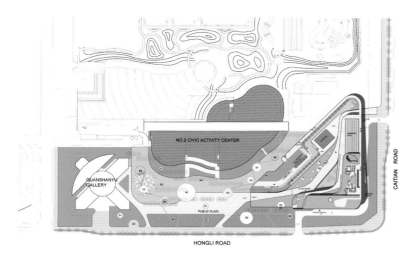

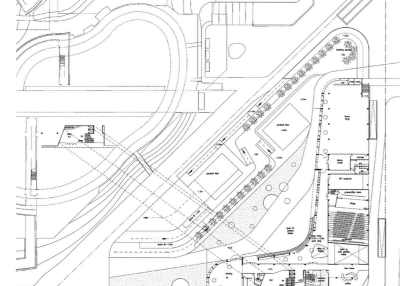

Located in a natural landscape reserve at the foot of Lotus Hill, the Senior Activity Center occupies a relatively unspoiled rural setting within the Shenzhen conurbation. The project is conceived as a gateway to a new city-centre area. Its 1.6-hectare site was originally planned as a highway intersection, which explains its triangular footprint abutting two major city thoroughfares. The architectural challenge was to integrate the new complex with neighbouring buildings while making the most of the triangular site's diagonal alignment to the adjacent meandering landscape.

The site was subject to various building constraints, such as a 17-metre height limit and 30% maximum plot coverage. The Shenzhen municipal government specified a programme comprising a multifunctional activity centre with sports, fitness and entertainment amenities as well as dining, meeting and cultural facilities, offices, classrooms and a range of outdoor sports activities.

The site is bounded on two sides by burgeoning city development, forming a stark contrast with its third edge, which is entirely open to the countryside. Its symbolic role at the threshold of the new city centre required a building with a distinctive urban character. As a counterpoint to the strict formality and monumentality of the urban planning next door, Open Architecture explored the idea of informality and freedom. They envisaged the Senior Activity Center as 'a programmed landscape' – a place for lively civic activities within a zone that straddles both natural and artificial realms. Architecture is used to negotiate the boundary of the city, between the rural and the synthetic.

Reiterating the contours of the landscape, green terraces retreat from the rolling hills towards the city's edge, pushing the building volume's centre of gravity towards the urban, where it increases in height and drama. The building gently emerges from the landscape, but is sheared off on the sides exposed to the forces of the city. Horizontal and vertical cut-outs are shaped into courtyards, sky-gardens and terraces, also encouraging cooling breezes to be sucked into the building.

Different types of planting create shade and regulate the microclimate. The south façade leans out, effectively blocking the high summer sun while permitting low winter sun to penetrate the building.

The centre was designed as an exemplary sustainable building, and geothermal cooling, grey-water recycling and solar panels are among the green technologies used in the project.

Opposite
The building is subtly terraced back from the landscape.

A sectional model and rendering show the inner courtyards, sky-gardens and terraces.

Above
The site and floor plans reveal how the building negotiates a fine line between nature and the city.

SHIPAI TOWN HALL, DONGGUAN, GUANGDONG

ATELIER FEICHANG JIANZHU, 2000–03

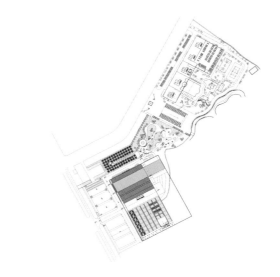

Located in the Pearl River Delta, Shipai is one of thirty-three townships dotted across Dongguan City. The town hall commissioned from Atelier Feichang Jianzhu by the Shipai Township Authority has a built area of 17,950 square metres. The region is renowned for its heat and humidity. Traditionally, its architecture has responded to these adverse conditions but, after air-conditioning became more prevalent in the area during the 1980s, climatically sensitive buildings have become a rarity. The architecture of Shipai's administrative centre addresses those deficiencies in a genuinely contextual manner.

From its front elevation the building looks like a single linear form, outlined by a slender white frame that is supported by a colonnade of columns with steps ascending to the entrance. Articulation gives the structure the solid, formal elegance that is expected of government buildings while providing efficient sunshading.

However, from the town hall's east and west elevations it becomes evident that the structure has been segmented and pulled apart. The slices, cut east to west, form three layers that allow the prevailing winds to filter through the open skeleton. The three slices vary in thickness according to the necessities of function and the adjacency of specific uses.

Natural ventilation cools the inner core of the building, making it comfortable for users. Simultaneously, the three segments are unified by a floating roof made of aluminium louvres on a steel frame. The horizontal louvres operate multifunctionally: as hot air rises it is expelled through the perforations; at the same time the glaring sunlight is moderated. Furthermore, the roof provides shelter and semi-enclosure to the intervening public spaces.

The large interstitial space forms a light corridor through the building, bringing sunshine and fresh air into the core offices. The ground rises as it penetrates the development through a series of gently rising stairs. These culminate in a horizontal platform that bridges the wings at their second level.

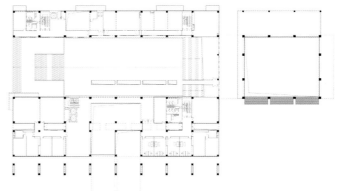

Right
The site plan, second-floor plan and the interwoven network of inner spaces highlight the building's open nature.

Opposite
The interstitial public space that separates two of the three segments brings light and air into the building.

The building appears as a single linear form from its front elevation.

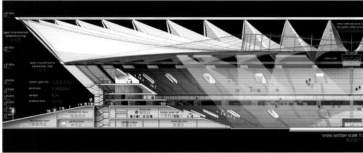

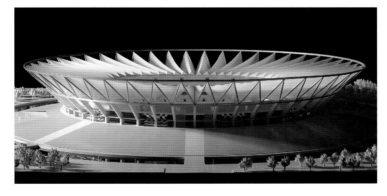

STADIUM WITH SPORTS PARK, FOSHAN, GUANGDONG

GMP – VON GERKAN, MARG UND PARTNER ARCHITECTS, 2003–06

Designed in time to meet the needs of the Twelfth Guangdong Province Sports Meeting in 2006, this multipurpose stadium gives Foshan a very modern sports centre. The facility will be seen as a symbol of the strength and influence of this increasingly prosperous province.

Forming the highlight of a large sports park, the stadium building sits in the heart of the landscape. The circular structure fulfils the architect's concept of a structure without direction and corresponds to the various facets of the surrounding urban development and open space.

The stadium emerges from the park in the form of a water lily blooming on a lake. Its situation on the brow of a hill creates a new landmark for the park and its adjacent river frontage. The park itself provides a green frame to the various sporting venues, including the stadium with its training courts, the swimming and high-diving

stadium with its open-air pools, and additional facilities such as parking areas and small pavilions.

The stadium's silhouette can be seen from a distance, its imposing monumental impact adding a recognizable image to the cityscape. The distinctive roof pattern unfurls like a flower. The white membrane, measuring 120 × 180 metres, is the biggest retractable roof in the world; in twelve minutes the roof can fold inwards to create a fully covered arena that completely shelters spectators from bad weather.

A large video cube floats above the centre of the sports field. The screens show the action – whether sports, cultural shows or concerts – to spectators in detail and from various perspectives. The cube also accommodates the inner roof membrane, an integrated approach that stretches its function beyond the conventional.

Opposite
The stadium is the centrepiece of a large sports park.

The inner roof of the circular structure is retractable.

Above
The 'water lily' effect of the roof form creates a memorable silhouette on the city skyline.

TIANJIN OLYMPIC CENTER STADIUM, NANKAI, TIANJIN

AXS SATOW, 2002–06

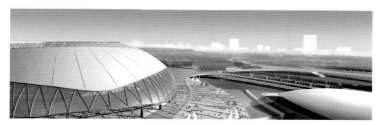

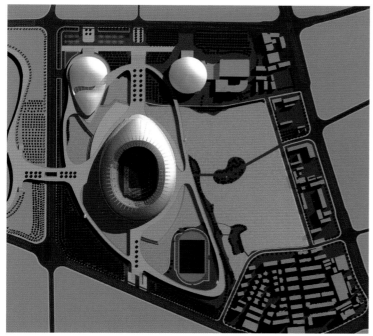

The project provides one of the major venues for the 2008 Beijing Olympic Games. The winning design, by AXS Satow in association with Tianjin Architects & Consulting Engineers, was selected after an invited international competition involving twelve prominent practices.

The site is subdivided into three zones: the Competition zone, the Xijie zone (a park) and the Xibeijie zone (containing the largest aquatic centre in Tianjin). The stadium occupies the heart of the Competition zone, the main focus for development. Historically, the city of Tianjin was known as a great water city, with abundant green spaces and rivers. With this in mind, the architects designed the stadium in the image of a droplet floating on the surface of water, creating a totally new glass architecture.

Other buildings on the site include the stadium built for the international table-tennis championships in 1995. There are also plans to construct a general-purpose stadium, an indoor swimming centre, an international sports-exchange centre, and various ancillary facilities. These too would be modelled using the water-drop form and linked by a loop-shaped pedestrian deck.

The three zones will all be connected via a looped circulation deck. This is not only intended to add dynamism to each zone, but also to provide convenient access from one to another. However, each pedestrian route invites a personal experience through different sequences of events.

The rounded droplet form of the stadium roof flows seamlessly into an artificial pond, blending quietly with the natural richness of the environment. The facility can be seen as representing a new ecological understanding of architecture, and a symbol for Tianjin in the new millennium. Constructed in steel with glass skylights, the roof simulates the mechanics of breathing skin, adapting itself to the sun, climate and wind conditions of the four seasons to provide optimum comfort for spectators and athletes.

Opposite

An aerial perspective emphasizes the concept of the stadium as a droplet surrounded by water.

A looped circulation deck links facilities.

Left

An aerial perspective shows the stadium site in the context of the city.

The plan outlines the relationship between the various facilities.

A rendering illustrates the spectator experience.

TIANTAI MUSEUM, ZHEJIANG

STUDIO WANG LU IN COLLABORATION WITH ZHEJIANG JIAJING
DESIGN & RESEARCH INSTITUTE, 1999–2003

The museum's site is rich in context, lying between Tiantai City and Tiantai Mountain to the west of the Guo Qing Temple. The Zhe Stream is immediately to the museum's east, and the land slopes by some 10 metres from the south-west edge up to the north-east corner.

The design began with two parallel concerns. As with any museum programme, the relationship between functions is highly significant, and the design brief was very specific in addressing the internal organization. However, the existing conditions of the area around the 1.7-hectare site were also paramount.

The architects questioned the homogenous spaces that commonly characterize exhibition halls, proposing instead to design the interiors according to the specific needs of the exhibits. Hence there are two types of exhibition accommodation: one is configured to showcase three-dimensional monumental exhibits such as statues and installations, while the other is dedicated to less bulky two-dimensional forms such as paintings and calligraphy. While the first requires volume, the second relies purely on surface. Addressing the brief's injunction to optimize the use of space, the architects developed a cross-frame and bearing-wall system in order to maximize the museum's vertical surfaces.

This interest in surface steered the design process towards an examination of how to streamline the structure and confront the external language of the building. Operationally, the connections between interior and exterior are ordered into three layers: roadside, core and riverside. Each of these layers is planned and interpreted differently in order to create a series of experiences. A path guides visitors from the road to the east, through the alternating weight and transparency of the museum spaces, before reaching the Zhe Stream at the western edge.

Above
The site plan establishes the clear boundaries of the museum.

Below
The museum's inner spaces are designated for different exhibitions, creating an unusual succession of experiences.

Opposite
Views from the exterior take in the picturesque Tiantai Mountain in the distance.

Inner courtyards and sunken water gardens inspire pause and reflection.

WATERCUBE NATIONAL SWIMMING CENTER, BEIJING OLYMPIC GREEN, BEIJING

PTW ARCHITECTS AND CSCEC-SDI, 2003–06

Following an international competition to design the 2008 Olympic Games National Swimming Center in July 2003, the commission was given to the team of PTW and CSCEC-SDI. Their highly praised Watercube concept won over the judges with its ability to meet international standards for competition while maximizing social and economic benefits.

The venue is designed to accommodate everything necessary for competitive indoor aquatic events as well as providing the public with multifunctional leisure and fitness facilities, both before and after the Olympics. The building adopts a simple square geometry; in doing so, the architects were inspired by the basic square plan of traditional Chinese houses and the symbolic role this geometry plays in the country's culture. However, it is the conglomeration of soap bubbles in foam that inspires the building's articulation. The architects describe the centre's association with water as a structural and conceptual 'leitmotif'.

Such an innovative scheme needed state-of-the-art technology and materials, not only to create the appropriate visual effect but also to comply with energy-efficiency and ecological requirements. The tailor-made lightweight framework that envelops the Watercube was developed by PTW and CSCEC-SDI with Arup. However, the seemingly random appearance of the façade is founded on a strict geometry that also characterizes the building blocks of many natural structures, such as crystals, cells and molecules. The system is the most efficient way of structuring three-dimensional space using uniformly sized components. Transparency and randomness is created by the application of inflated ETFE cushions to the inner and outer façade skins.

Conventional stadium structures have gigantic columns and beams, cables and spans, to which a façade system is applied. With the Watercube, the architectural space, structure and cladding are unified as a single element. The concept of a 'cube of water bubbles' is translated from the square box into its internal planning. The series of interior spaces seems to be sculpted out of the unconfined mass of foam bubbles, a state that the architects feel symbolizes "a condition of nature that is transformed into a condition of culture".

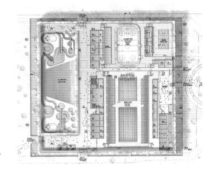

Above
The floor plan reveals the internal organization of the centre.

Below
The aptly named Watercube is wrapped in an integrated structural façade system that emulates soap bubbles.

Opposite
The water-sports venue is located close to the main Olympic Stadium.

WUKESONG CULTURAL AND SPORTS CENTER, HAI DIAN, BEIJING

BURCKHARDT+PARTNER, 2003–08

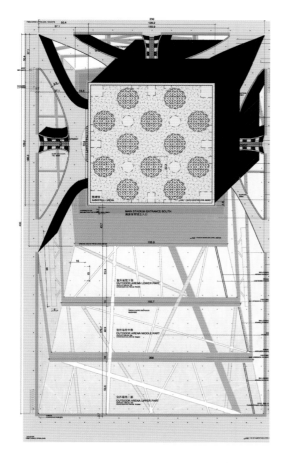

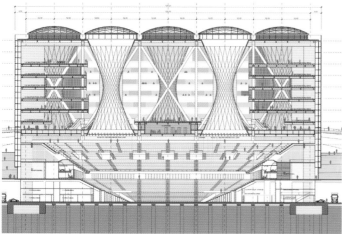

Following an international competition for the conceptual planning and design of the Wukesong Cultural and Sports Center, the first prize was awarded to Burckhardt+Partner. The 50-hectare project, conceived as a park in which people can immerse themselves, is designed as a series of crater arenas that invite participation. This planning strategy seeks to maximize the options for flexible development, unifying the site and enhancing its horizontal openness.

During the Olympic Games, the Wukesong Arena that is contained within the centre will host the basketball championship. Afterwards, the development will become a broad-based leisure venue, hosting cultural, social and sports events, including concerts, theatre, outdoor cinema screenings, trade fairs and expositions. Commercial activities are expected to be integrated when the demand arises.

Upper and lower horizontal planes of activity range from playing and sports fields to wild parks and avenues. The raised levels form a well-defined circulation grid, linking with the transport network and providing views of the activities taking place below. The lower plane is perceived as changeable, with the capacity to adapt to new needs.

A network of audio-visual installations, designed as 'sound islands', will enable spectators to enjoy films and events broadcast on giant screens occupying the four façades of the Wukesong Arena building. Sound can also be accessed all over the park through wireless transmission systems and earphones.

The arena has a floor area of 106,000 square metres and accommodates a multifunctional hall with a seating capacity of 18,000. The upper portion features more than 60,000 square metres of commercial uses, enlivening the arena and increasing the economic benefits of the project. Natural ventilation is generated by the geometry and design of the building. Twelve hyperbolic paraboloids hang from the main structure and support any loads placed over the stadium. They also act as chimneys, maximizing heating and air-conditioning savings by drawing exterior air from the lower part and expelling it throughout the upper part.

Opposite
The arena sits within expansive parkland, its façades transformed into giant projection screens for the entertainment of users.

The structure is perforated by paraboloids that promote natural ventilation through the building.

Left
The site plan reveals the structural loads of the arena building, supported by twelve hanging paraboloids.

A cross-section shows the framework of the arena. Its fixed upper framework forms a clear circulation grid, while the flexible lower layer adapts to different uses.

YILANZHAI ART MUSEUM, NANJING

KISHO KUROKAWA ARCHITECT & ASSOCIATES, 2003–05 (PHASE ONE)

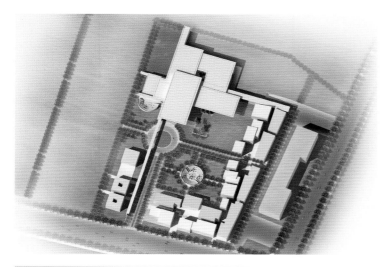

The Yilanzhai Art Museum takes its inspiration from the qualities of the surroundings, most notably the Chang Jiang River, the Qin Huai River, Lake Xuan Wu and the abundant bamboo forests. This rich natural heritage, as well as the image of the city walls and tiled roofs, provided a starting point from which the architecture emerges. The museum will house traditional Chinese arts, but also has the capacity to function as a multipurpose international museum, hosting public exhibitions, art auctions and events.

Japanese architect Kisho Kurokawa is renowned for his work analysing the idea of a new world order. This is documented in his *The Philosophy of Symbiosis*, and the architecture for Yilanzhai Art Museum embodies the theme. Poetic references are reinterpreted symbolically by Kurokawa, with a modern architectural sensibility. He takes four walls to define four distinct areas of the museum and accords them different functions. The south-east wall is instrumental in forming the façade, a plaza and, for visitors, a clear route to the entrance. To the south-west an area is designated for a gallery and craft workshops. In the north-east corner the service area incorporates a loading and unloading entrance as well as car parking and staff access. Lastly, the north-west area primarily contains an exhibition space. Air-conditioning, lighting, management and security systems use the most sophisticated technology, much of which has not previously been specified in China.

Elements of the architecture, such as the horizontally overlapping roof profiles, create rhythm and fluidity. They not only provide accent and movement but also capture and manipulate natural light and shadow, drawing them inside through the subtle seams in the architecture. The pond surrounding the building forms a symbiotic relationship with the museum, its surface finding precisely the same level as the floor of the building. The two entities coexist in perfect harmony.

Columns randomly positioned to support the canopy of the front entrance plaza are conceived as a metaphor of the bamboo forests. Except for the storage and exhibition halls, public space is denoted by transparent glazing so that inside and out is experienced as a continuum, assimilated with nature.

Opposite
Rhythm and fluidity are expressed by the architecture, from the front entrance plaza to the reflecting pond.

Left
An aerial rendering reveals the organization of different functions.

Interior circulation is modulated with natural light and shadow.

CONVENTION CENTRES AND TRANSPORTATION

BEIJING CAPITAL INTERNATIONAL AIRPORT, BEIJING
FOSTER AND PARTNERS

BEIJING INTERNATIONAL AUTOMOTIVE EXPO CENTER, FENG TAI, BEIJING
HENN ARCHITEKTEN

BEIJING NATIONAL OLYMPIC GREEN CONVENTION CENTRE, OLYMPIC BOULEVARD, BEIJING
RMJM HK

BENGBU CITY CENTRAL PLAZA, BENGBU CITY, ANHUI
PTW ARCHITECTS

GUANGZHOU INTERNATIONAL CONVENTION & EXHIBITION CENTRE, GUANGZHOU
AXS SATOW

GUANGZHOU NEW BAIYUN AIRPORT, GUANGZHOU
PARSONS/URS GREINER/GUANGDONG PROVINCIAL ARCHITECTURAL DESIGN INSTITUTE

LONGGANG EXHIBITION CENTER, SHENZHEN
URBANUS ARCHITECTURE AND DESIGN

NANNING INTERNATIONAL CONFERENCE & EXHIBITION CENTER, NANNING
GMP – VON GERKAN, MARG UND PARTNER ARCHITECTS

QINGDAO AIRPORT, QINGDAO
WOODHEAD INTERNATIONAL

SHANGHAI INTERNATIONAL EXPO CENTRE, PUDONG, SHANGHAI
MURPHY/JAHN

SHENZHEN CONVENTION AND EXHIBITION CENTER, SHENZHEN
GMP – VON GERKAN, MARG UND PARTNER ARCHITECTS

XINGTAO EXHIBITION AND RECEPTION CENTER, DAXING, BEIJING
CHINA ARCHITECTURE DESIGN & RESEARCH GROUP

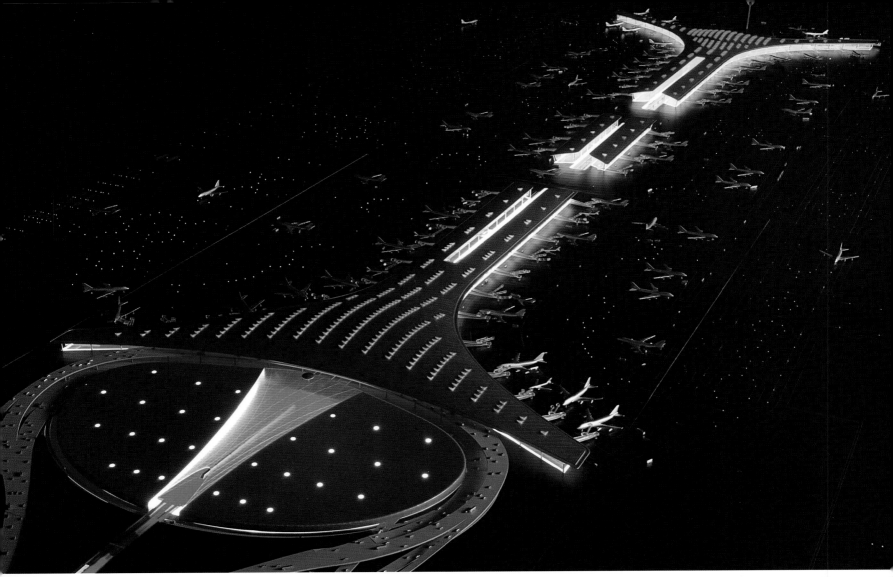

BEIJING CAPITAL INTERNATIONAL AIRPORT, BEIJING

FOSTER AND PARTNERS, 2003–07

Beijing Capital International Airport will help to meet the rapid expansion in travel anticipated after China's entry in the World Trade Organization and for the 2008 Olympics. Foster and Partners' new terminal and masterplan is conceived as a people's palace that celebrates flight and evokes a sense of place.

This is Foster's largest and most innovative airport to date, with a design and construction programme spanning just four years. Rooted in the airport paradigm pioneered by the firm at Stansted in 1991 and Chek Lap Kok in 1998, the architecture combines spatial clarity with a highly functional system for processing an estimated 44 million passengers a year. Given the unpredictable nature of the aviation industry, the plan follows a seamless layout that is designed for maximum flexibility, with the longer-term goal of reaching an annual capacity of 53 million passengers.

Using the traditional Chinese colours of red and yellow (imperial colours signifying royalty and nobility and often associated with Beijing), the terminal is designed to respond to the city's identity, providing a true sense of arrival and, in due course, becoming a national icon. Its dragon-like form accommodates the new terminal area along its central axis, which sits between the existing eastern runway and a third runway that will be built later.

Despite the soaring aerodynamic form of the building, there are relatively few level changes for passengers to negotiate. The lofty roof sailing over the entire terminal filters the sunlight, creating a sense of place and aiding orientation through its linear rooflights.

Sustainability is incorporated into the airport design: the south-east-facing skylights capitalize on heat gain from the early-morning sun, and an integrated environmental-control system minimizes energy consumption and carbon emissions.

The new terminal will take on a civic role as an important public building, where large numbers of people find their way in an environment that suggests the poetry of flight and makes the complexities of modern travel easy to understand, with invisible but highly efficient processing systems.

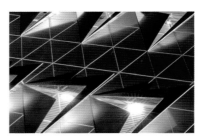

Opposite
Aerial visualizations of the new airport terminal emphasize its soaring roof form.

Left
A plan of the terminal building reveals its spatial clarity from land- to airside.

The skylights take advantage of the heat gained from the morning sun.

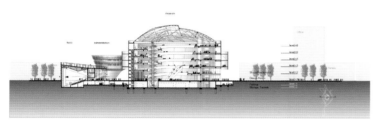

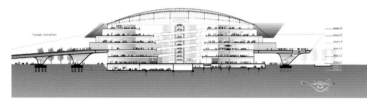

BEIJING INTERNATIONAL AUTOMOTIVE EXPO CENTER, FENG TAI, BEIJING

HENN ARCHITEKTEN, 2003–07

Sited on the Fourth Ring Road in the city's south-west quarter, the Beijing International Automotive Expo Center is one of many world-class venues scheduled for completion before the 2008 Olympic Games. Henn Architekten from Germany was awarded the project after winning an international competition held in 2003.

The diversity of automobile travel is depicted in a lively journey outlining the development of the car from its origins, showcased in the Automobile Museum. The experience continues to the present-day, where car manufacturers are brought together in the Brand Pavilions. Finally, the Auto University displays research into prototypical vehicles of the future. The arrangement of the buildings, their associated functions and the topography of the site are designed around this basic programme.

The Automobile Museum is the spatial and contextual nerve centre of the Museum Plaza. While conveying the essence of more than a century of automobile history, in urban-planning terms the space serves as the formal entrance to the Beijing

International Automotive Expo Center. The core facility is accompanied by supporting activities such as a services building for the car manufacturers, showrooms for brands and garages with workshops. Other complementary uses, including hotels, shopping malls and residential buildings, are also planned. In the middle of the exhibition grounds there is a geometric reference to the Forbidden City in the form of a rectangular theme park, which contains the Brand Pavilions.

The amorphous form of the museum's exterior is sleekly contoured in metallic cladding. Internally, five floors are linked to a spacious, light-flooded atrium. Individual floors are connected by curved stairwells, open stairs and lifts. Encircling the void, a spiralling circulation system feeds into gallery spaces. The highly fluid spaces can also be subdivided, providing the high degree of flexibility required by potential users.

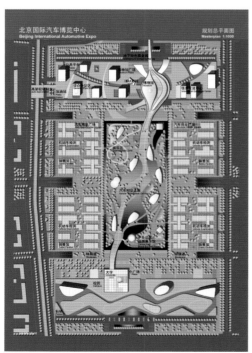

Opposite
An aerial rendering reveals the museum's amorphous form.

Pedestrian circulation bridges over a landscaped boulevard, while the internal atrium is encircled by flexible exhibition spaces.

Left
The floor plan and longitudinal and cross-sections emphasize the extruded connecting nodes.

The masterplan shows the major components of the site.

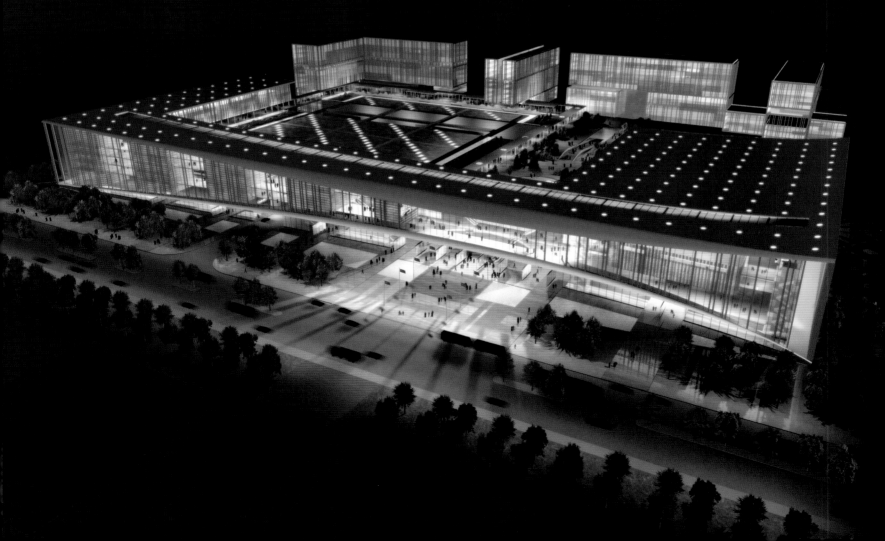

BEIJING NATIONAL OLYMPIC GREEN CONVENTION CENTRE, OLYMPIC BOULEVARD, BEIJING

RMJM HK, 2004–07

RMJM was commissioned to design the Beijing Olympic Green Convention Centre after an invited competition organized by the client, Beijing North Star, involving several prominent overseas practices. The 12.2-hectare masterplan incorporates the design of the 220,000-square-metre convention centre as well as a further 260,000 square metres of commercial, retail and hotel accommodation.

Located in a prominent position on Olympic Boulevard, close to key sporting venues including the National Stadium and the Watercube swimming complex, the centre will stage four separate sporting events in two 5000-seat venues with the back-up facilities required for Olympic-class events. However, adding to the complexity of the brief, it also has to accommodate the 84,000-square-metre Olympic press and broadcasting centre, providing facilities for the world's media.

After the games the convention centre and its associated mixed-use development will become a vital commercial and entertainment hub in Beijing's Olympics-driven urban-regeneration plans. In order to ensure sustainability, flexible planning has been crucial.

After the Olympics the building will accommodate multiple conventions. The plenary hall can hold 6000 people and uses both retractable seating and moveable 13-metre-high partitions to make a wide range of convention activities possible.

The concept of unity provided the principal theme, embracing the spirit of the games as well as the philosophy of the Olympic Green masterplan. A strategic balance between commercial accommodation and public amenities is planned around the environmentally friendly Central Garden Plaza situated above the retail podium, providing a direct link to the hotel and office components of the project.

Opposite
Perspectives highlight both the convention and mixed-use aspects of the project.

The glazed façade provides an animated edge facing Olympic Boulevard.

Above
Natural light penetrates the internal circulation routes of the complex, offering visitors open views of the Olympic landscape.

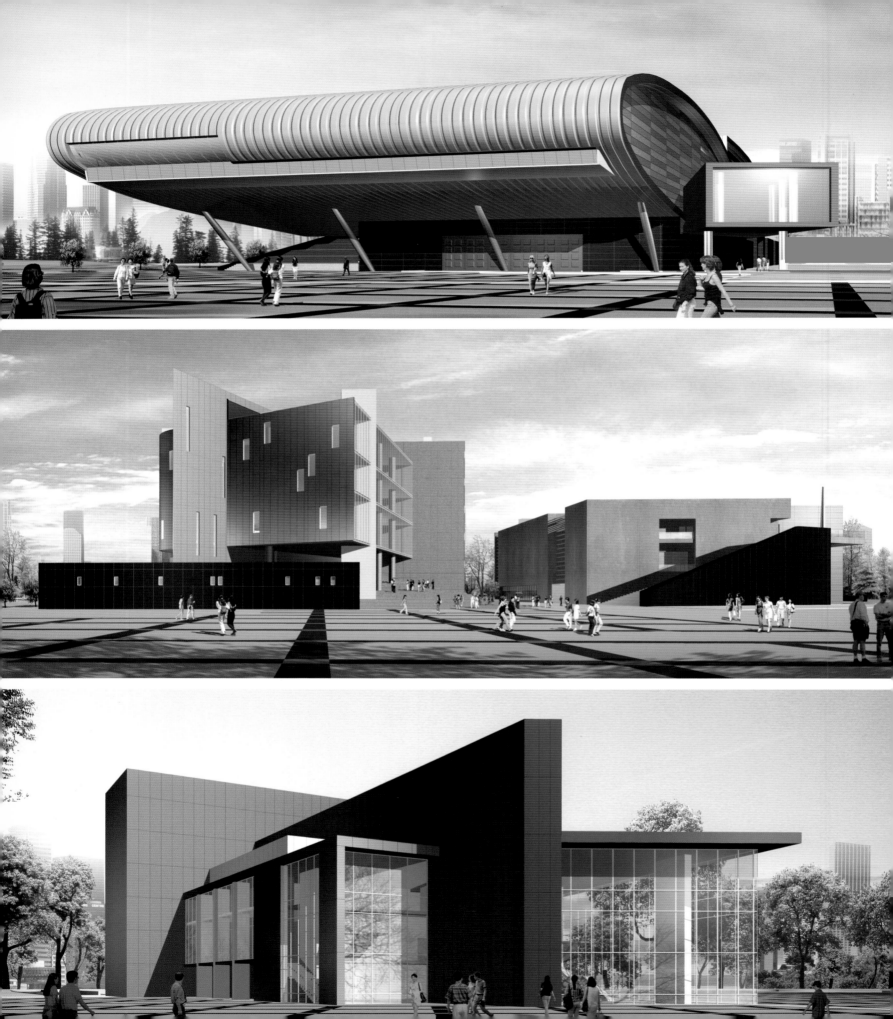

BENGBU CITY CENTRAL PLAZA, BENGBU CITY, ANHUI

PTW ARCHITECTS, 2001–04

Opposite
There are five distinct architectural components within the programme's mix of cultural, hospitality and commercial uses.

Right
The masterplan of the site demonstrates how the different facilities are woven together.

The opening of the new Bengbu City Central Plaza marks a watershed in the fast-track development of the metropolis. The purpose of the project – provision of much-needed convention and exhibition space – indicates the level of maturity that the city has reached.

However, apart from the business of forums and trade shows, the project's programme was heavily weighted towards civic functions, requiring the integration of a theatre, library, museum and leisure centre. The complex blend of uses – mixing cultural and commercial, hospitality and educational, arts and recreation – called for a sensitive approach, and PTW Architects, a Sydney-based practice,

orchestrated an unusual solution.

There are five major components, with a total built area of 40,000 square metres. Each component presented its own challenges. For instance, the theatre had to be designed as a multifunctional arena, and the museum's focus on science and technology added to the complexity of the programme. The 20,000-square-metre exhibition centre was subject to site-cover limitations, so the large halls had to be distributed over two levels.

The distinctive structures are strategically orientated around an open plaza, providing vital open space for the local community. The architects scoured journals and archival research on Bengbu

to bring a sense of historic value to the project. The result combines elements of Bengbu's legendary past, such as the story of Da Yu and the control of the flood, with rational, modern design.

Facilities have been meticulously knitted together efficiently and flexibly to accommodate changes that the client might require in the future. Each function relies on the integral role played by the landscaping. Buildings and their surroundings are closely complementary, ensuring that they work interdependently. Tying them together not only enhances the sense of a civic gathering space but also tackles problems of circulation and linkage.

GUANGZHOU INTERNATIONAL CONVENTION & EXHIBITION CENTRE, GUANGZHOU

AXS SATOW, 1999–2003

The proposal for the convention and exhibition centre was chosen after an invited international competition. The selection process involved twelve architectural practices: seven overseas and five Chinese firms. The facility was built in south-eastern Guangzhou on a generous 70-hectare site, from the north end of which the Zhujiang River flows. 'Piao', meaning breeze, provides the motif for the architecture, reflecting the riverine scenery. The building embraces its waterfront environment by intertwining the river and the exhibition halls with an architecture that is intended to float like a breeze. The architects chose a soft metal to represent the ripples of the wind, but the building is primarily envisaged as a new symbol of modern architecture for the city of Guangzhou.

Throughout the interior and exterior spaces in the complex, pedestrian and vehicular-circulation routes are clearly separated and demarcated to form a convenient urban network. The Pearl Promenade on the second level is designed as the central pedestrian path; from here all the floors and exhibition/convention areas are easily accessible. The promenade also feeds into the external pedestrian deck that leads to the surrounding facilities.

Responding to the natural elements of the Zhujiang River, the building, with its themes of light, wind, water and green open space, is a showcase of various ecologically sensitive principles. A glass-walled lobby runs through the centre of the complex along an east–west axis parallel to the river. This serves as the main space for social exchange and circulation. A curtain wall built of low-e glass provides the envelope for a three-storey lobby area, the surface of which is also used as signage. Visitors and exhibitors are welcomed into this 25 × 450-metre space from which they can take in the scenery of the riverscape before making their way to the exhibition halls.

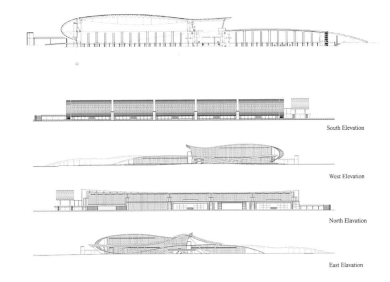

South Elevation

West Elevation

North Elevation

East Elevation

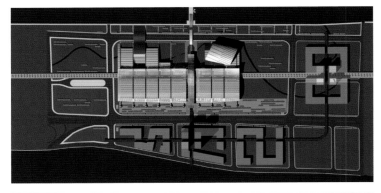

Right
A section and elevations show the inter-relationship of various functions.

The site plan shows the complex's position on the waterfront.

The view from the river reveals the facility's spacious site.

Opposite
A soft metal wave-like canopy structure envelops the building, creating a snaking form that emulates the river breezes and brings light into the main lobby space.

GUANGZHOU NEW BAIYUN AIRPORT, GUANGZHOU

PARSONS/URS GREINER/GUANGDONG PROVINCIAL
ARCHITECTURAL DESIGN INSTITUTE, 1999–2004

Conceived as a major gateway to China, this collaborative architectural and construction effort between US and Chinese counterparts provides the increased capacity the region needs. The team was responsible for the first-phase conceptual design of the passenger-terminal layout, including landside functions and services. With project approval granted by the Civil Aviation Administration of China and the China State Development and Planning Commission in the 1990s, the final scheme covers 13.5 km – five times the size of the former airport – and is capable of handling 25 million passengers annually.

The architecture encompasses the main terminal, the east–west connection building, four concourses, landscaped surface parking, structured parking, an airport hotel, and the tallest air-traffic-control tower in the country. This first phase also included two runways, aircraft-maintenance and air-cargo facilities, over sixty aircraft hardstands, vehicle parking, and a new highway and rail system serving the airport. Included in the plans are two terminal-area loop roadway systems to facilitate landside traffic flow and reduce congestion, and a metro rail station for travel to downtown Guangzhou located under the terminal.

At its height, construction of the airy glass and steel structure involved more than 10,000 workers, and 20,000 people had to be relocated to make room for the massive project.

When fully operational, the airport will house an international-standard convention centre where visitors can arrive by plane, check into a quality hotel, eat, shop, and attend a conference – all without having to leave the airport. An area covering 200,000 square metres is set aside for shopping facilities, a hotel with up to 800 rooms, a convention centre and exhibition halls.

Below
A logical sequence of functions occupies the expansive halls of the airport terminal, defined by a soaring skylit roof.

Opposite
The new airport was designed as a gateway to China. It is capable of handling 186,000 aircraft operations annually.

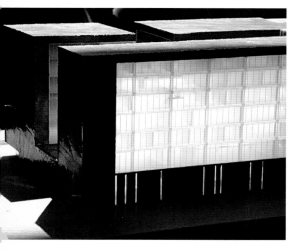

LONGGANG EXHIBITION CENTER, SHENZHEN

URBANUS ARCHITECTURE AND DESIGN, 2000–06

As an architectural genre, exhibition centres are typically bulky, having to provide the large capacity required by trade-fair halls and the high volume of traffic attending events, and immense back-of-house infrastructural support. Urbanus approached the Longgang Exhibition Center from a very different perspective. Obvious inspirational sources might have included airports or shopping centres, but Urbanus was struck by the residential typology of the local area.

Extreme in its sense of paradox, this angle was nevertheless pursued by the architects by exploring the internal logic shared by modern architectural language and traditional community forms. Traditionally, the courtyard exists as a direct response to local culture and climate, and in the Longgang region it is the principal element that defines architectural space. The design concept for the Longgang Exhibition Center interprets a similar spatial system, albeit on a grander scale.

In its role as space organizer, the courtyard is particularly efficient. It allows the convergence of public, semi-public and private spaces through a hierarchy of scales that extend horizontally. Unfortunately, the limitations of the site's footprint did not permit the architects to adopt this traditional language fully. However, a similar relationship is established by designing a vertical sequence of courtyards.

At various levels of the building, segments are carved out to create voids at different scales and with various perspectives. Each has an individual identity, helping to orientate users, and is endowed with a particular role. The openings weave into each other and overlap at strategic points. They also offer shelter from glaring sun and heavy rain, making them fully functional all year round.

The supporting office spaces are placed on the north-east elevation, where the façade is clad with a greater proportion of glass, maximizing the penetration of natural light while avoiding solar gain. The glassy surface dissolves the bulkiness of the structure, blurring the edges and reflecting the surrounding trees.

Opposite
An exterior view of the exhibition centre emphasizes its carved-out façade.

Different perspectives of the model highlight the sequence of courtyard spaces.

Above
The inner plazas allow various functions to converge.

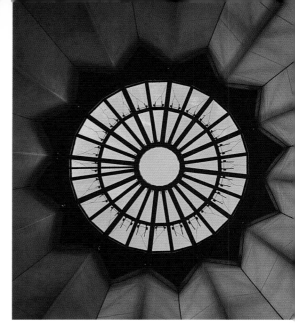

NANNING INTERNATIONAL CONFERENCE & EXHIBITION CENTER, NANNING

GMP – VON GERKAN, MARG UND PARTNER ARCHITECTS, 1999–2005

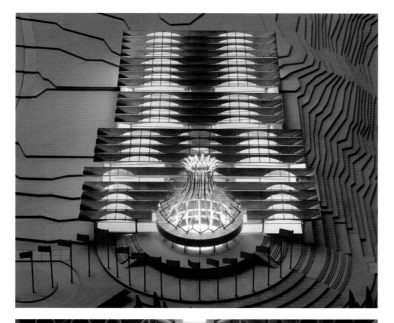

The sloping site, with a height difference of about 45 metres from end to end, inspired an unusual form for the Nanning International Conference & Exhibition Center. Its hillside location lends the building a degree of prominence, and its cosmopolitan architectural language reflects the rapidly growing metropolis of which it has become part. This effect is emphasized by the presence of a large chimney-like structure on axis with the city centre. The translucent fluted cone suggests a blossoming flower, and provides a stunning symbolic image for the city.

The building is designed to host trade fairs and conferences. Access is via a pedestrian bridge from the exhibition square. As users enter the complex, escalators and a wide, gently rising staircase take them to the four multiple-use exhibition halls and a spacious forecourt. A single roof structure shelters all these components. The exhibition spaces are positioned along both sides of the two-storey foyer and all can be linked in flexible ways to operate in combination.

A larger exhibition hall has an overall height of 70 metres and a diameter of 48 metres. The multifunctional space crowned with the lantern-like structure is plugged into the far end of the site, where the slope flattens out. Its prominent position and outlook make it a perfect venue for high-profile events. As it protrudes from the head of the complex, the hall's silhouette creates an identifiable landmark across the city.

The faceted cone has a tapering filigree-steel framework. This is covered in a thermally insulating translucent fabric membrane that filters a comfortable level of natural light into the exhibition space below. At night the cone is illuminated from within, radiating a diffuse glow across the city and its surrounding area.

Opposite
Illuminated at night, the convention centre projects a distinctive form towards the city.

The lantern-like cone crowns the larger multifunctional space, its faceted composition creating an intriguing counterpoint to the other halls.

Left
An aerial view of the model emphasizes its hilltop location.

The exhibition halls are disposed around a cavernous foyer space that is filled with natural light.

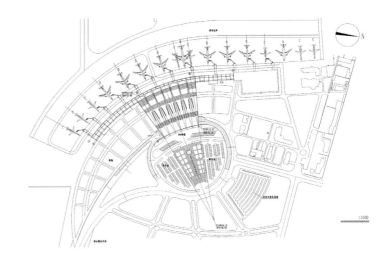

QINGDAO AIRPORT, QINGDAO

WOODHEAD INTERNATIONAL, 2000–04

Qingdao's coastal location provided the inspiration for the design of its new airport terminal. The building's soft curving forms and the extensive use of natural sandstone convey the physical movement between earth and sky that defines the essence of an airport's purpose.

Viewed from outside the mammoth arched roof resembles the contours of a seashell. The effect is translated to the interior as expansive light-filled spaces, from the check-in halls to the departure gates. Travellers experience a heightened awareness of natural light and the building's vast size through the glass ribs that span from one end of the building to the other.

The check-in halls are organized as islands within the space, reducing pedestrian congestion. When passengers have finished checking-in, areas of generously comfortable seating, unusual

in airport-furniture design, are intended to relieve stress.

Passengers are able to cross-reference their position and orientate themselves from any part of the terminal, something that is vitally important in an internal landscape as large as this. Travellers are also given views of the departure gates. The focus is on extending visibility: shops are clearly delineated, while perimeter seating provides ample space, away from primary circulation routes, where passengers can simply take in the stunning views of the city.

Airports are not merely gateways; they also mark a city's status and celebrate its modernity. For Qingdao, the airport serves as an emblem of the metropolis and the surrounding area. It is designed to exceed international standards of air travel and incorporates themes that capture the natural beauty of the region without resorting to the literal.

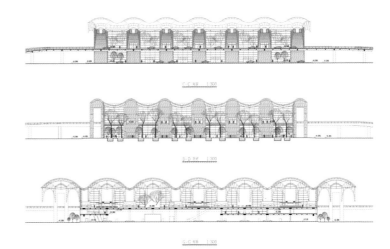

Above
The masterplan of the airport site and sections through the terminal building reveal its soft curving forms and waved roof structure.

Opposite
A ribbed colonnade arches over the highway, marking the main entrance to the terminal.

An overriding sense of space and light characterizes the vast halls.

SHANGHAI INTERNATIONAL EXPO CENTRE, PUDONG, SHANGHAI

MURPHY/JAHN, 1998–2002

Built for a consortium of German trade-fair organizations (Messe Munich, Messe Düsseldorf, Hannover Fairs) in a joint venture with the Shanghai Pudong Development Company, the architecture for the International Expo Centre in Pudong derives its conceptual base from urban planning. Murphy/Jahn has created a town centre with an open plaza flanked by exhibition halls in a triangular diagram. Entrances penetrate the points of the triangle, and covered arcades tie the circulation and halls together. The modular structures of the exhibition spaces create a repeated and subtle wave effect, enhancing the development's identity in the city.

The programme was conducted in phases, the first comprising four exhibition halls with an open exhibition area and an entrance hall. A taller exhibition venue was added in the second phase.

A circular tower at the north-west corner adjacent to the congress centre marks the main entrance to the fairgrounds. The structure accommodates offices and a 400-room hotel. A linear progression of spaces begins with the drive, entrance hall, arcade and the five halls, woven together to present a coherent image.

At both ends of the mammoth halls (measuring 68 × 164 metres) are core zones with shops facing the arcade. Restaurants are inserted above the cores of the second and third halls with catering facilities also occupying the linking space. With column-free interiors and clear heights of 11 metres (17 metres in the taller hall), there is flexibility for truck access, floor loading, utilities, toilets, food and beverage facilities, conference rooms and crate storage. Energy-use and comfort are major issues, and the short occupancy times during events have had to be taken into account. Natural conditions prevail during setting-up and dismantling.

The structural framework of the roof is a system of supported steel girders with 72-metre centre spans and modest cantilevers at either end. Each girder consists of an upper and lower steel beam with V-shaped posts connecting the two to form a diamond in section. The girder's profile along the span follows the bending-moment diagram, creating a remarkably lightweight and elegant composition. The upper steel components also form the crescent-shaped ridge that receives the translucent fabric cladding. Along the roof's longitudinal cantilevered edge runs a hollow steel box resembling an aircraft wing. This forms a crisp edge to the building while transferring the girders' compressive forces to the columns' axis, where cables are fixed and lateral stiffness to the roof plane is provided.

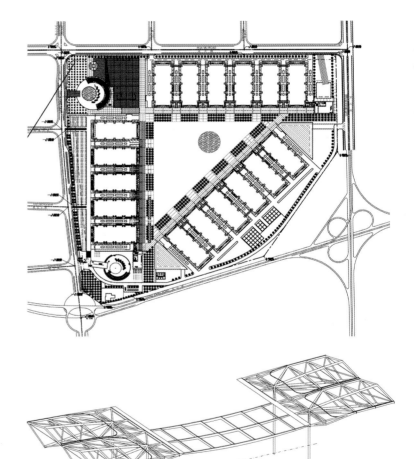

Right
The footprint of the complex reveals the triangular arrangement of the exhibition halls.

The structural framework of the roof comprises a system of supported steel girders.

Opposite
Entrances penetrate the points of the triangular site.

The canopied roof edge of the buildings creates a coherent form.

SHENZHEN CONVENTION AND EXHIBITION CENTER, SHENZHEN

GMP – VON GERKAN, MARG UND PARTNER ARCHITECTS, 2001–05

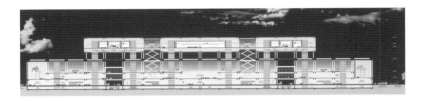

With its exhibition ground complete and a convention centre due to open in 2005, the thriving city of Shenzhen is looking forward to hosting international trade shows and forums of the highest calibre. The programme for the new Shenzhen Convention and Exhibition Center (SZCEC) called for much more than simply a building for trade fairs and conferences. Its complex nature entailed a synthesis of urban planning, architecture and construction in order to achieve an integrated structure with an urban density.

Nestled between numerous high-rise towers, the total exhibition area spans a single level with a rectangular plan of 280 × 540 metres. Access is via an elevated entrance and visitor platform located 7.5 metres above street level. This permits segregated circulation to single halls or combined hall complexes. Raising the entrance was also deemed necessary in order completely to separate visitor circulation through the central axis of the halls from exhibitors' logistic systems. The configuration adopted allows the optional allocation of entrance and exit points to the halls below while maintaining clear orientation and layout for users.

Along the central spine of the building, large steel trestle structures, A-shaped in section, are inserted at 30-metre intervals and rise to almost 60 metres. These structures support the congress building, 360 metres long, 60 metres wide and 20 metres high, which hovers 15 metres above the exhibition halls. The components are stiffened in the framework and are interconnected to provide mutual stability.

The congress building is a tube-like composition. Suspended above the halls, it affords remarkable flexibility in use. The spaces can be operated either as separate units, or at 50% of capacity, or in tandem with the exhibition area. Stretching over 540 metres, the SZCEC evokes progressive predecessors such as London's famous Crystal Palace, home of the Great Exhibition in 1851, and is double the length of the large glass hall of the 1996 Leipzig Exhibition Centre.

During the day, the glass vault covering the nine exhibition halls gives the impression of a delicate sculpture, while at night it radiates like a crystal. The entrance square is animated with illuminated fountains and water cascades, and coloured lighting effects add a vibrant glow to the congress centre above.

Above
A section shows the exhibition area with the congress building suspended above.

Below
An outdoor plaza leads to the elevated entrance and glass-fronted foyer.

Opposite
Aerial views show the enormous exhibition grounds anchored in the highly urban context of Shenzhen.

XINGTAO EXHIBITION AND RECEPTION CENTER, DAXING, BEIJING

CHINA ARCHITECTURE DESIGN & RESEARCH GROUP, 2001

Located at the gateway to a residential project currently being developed in an exclusive Beijing suburb, the Xingtao Exhibition and Reception Center is a stunning showcase for visitors. Its modest elegance and tranquility are intended to convey the high-quality standards offered by the planned residential project.

The facility integrates various commercial functions. The relationships between these are confronted in a manner that is sensitive to traditional Oriental influences in terms of spatial hierarchy and experience. The architects understand the cultural subtleties of using locally sourced modern materials and of applying these with current technologies in order to construct a genuinely contemporary piece of architecture. Services are thus offered in a modern setting yet delivered in ways that are sympathetic to cultural tradition.

One of the guiding principles of the project is the strategic placing of wall features, intended to assist circulation through the building. The configuration holds special significance, originating in the architectural traditions of China, expressed particularly in the formal structures of its classical gardens.

Despite a tight budget and the speed at which the project had to be implemented, the architects have woven the building around a series of tranquil gardens, intimately connecting them through an extended canopy. The two major landscapes form an outer pool and inner courtyard garden, each tied into the experience of the interior spaces.

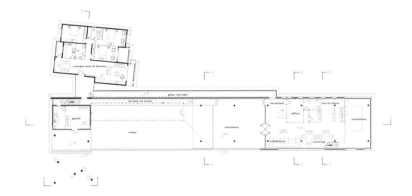

Left, above and opposite
Serving as an imposing gateway to a residential development, the reception centre is built around a series of tranquil gardens, connected by an overhanging canopy.

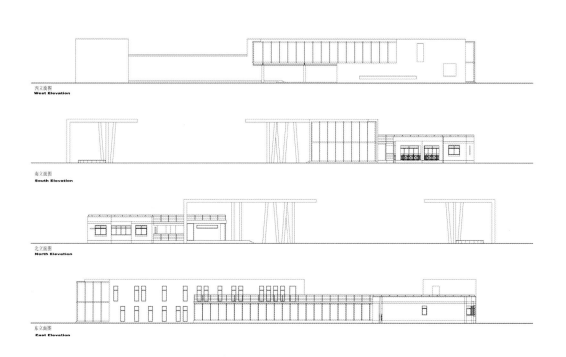

西立面图
West Elevation

南立面图
South Elevation

北立面图
North Elevation

东立面图
East Elevation

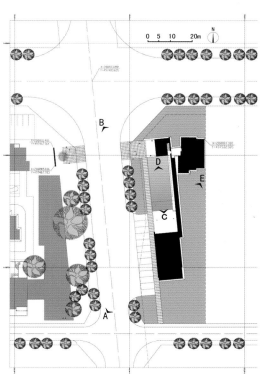

0 5 10   20m   N

B

D

E

C

A

HOUSES AND HOUSING

AIRPORT HOUSE, COMMUNE-BY-THE-WALL, BEIJING

CHIEN HSUEH-YI, 2000–02

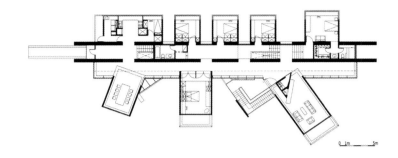

The plan of this 603-square-metre, three-storey building reveals the inspiration for its name, although this may not have been what Chien Hsueh-Yi had in mind when he conceived his house. No doubt the people staying here have sat in many airport terminals, probably in the business-class lounge, and may find it vaguely familiar.

The architect responded first to the conditions of the site, particularly its special historical and environmental significance. The steel and concrete villa, one of eleven commissioned from different Asian architects by the entrepreneurial developer Redstone Industrie, is intended to blend with the landscape and encourage those staying there to be close to nature. The plan is clearly readable, following the linearity of the Great Wall. The layout is determined by a spinal double wall that distributes the various domestic functions along either side of its length.

One of the most striking aspects of the stone wall of the spine is its axis across the steeply sloping site, a marked contrast. Besides the wall's metaphorical alliance with the Great Wall, the architect suggests it resembles an animal's spinal column.

Living, dining and bedroom spaces are plugged into the wall, some at different angles, and cantilevered on stilts. Within these 'pods' it is possible to become completely immersed in the starkness of the surrounding hillsides. Public domains such as the living and dining spaces cling to a light-filled corridor, while bedrooms, bathrooms, kitchen and service areas are slotted into the inner passageway, which is lined with grey stone. Like walking inside the Great Wall, this rear corridor feels solid and secure. It is constructed from stone collected from the site, so the analogy is evident. However, it is lifted by the skylight that draws shafts of sunlight into the circulation space.

Above
As in the case of the departure gates at an airport terminal, the Airport House plan clearly reveals the plugged-in domestic spaces.

Below
The double circulation spine creates an interplay between solid and void.

Opposite
The axis of the villa cuts across the steep incline of the hills, creating a stark contrast with the ground plane.

BAMBOO HOUSE, COMMUNE-BY-THE-WALL, BEIJING

KENGO KUMA, 2000–02

The composition of this two-storey, 716-square-metre house develops from two major concerns. Kengo Kuma wanted to learn from the external construction methods of the Great Wall, specifically its seamless integration with the topography, as opposed to the creation of an isolated object on a level site. In parallel, he confronted the issue of the building's delicacy in terms of the intrinsic ruggedness of the landscape.

The house perches on the untreated slopes of a narrow ridge with open views across the valley. Rather than modifying the site in order to create a contrast between it

and the building, Kuma does the opposite. Just as the rugged nature of the landscape surrounding the Great Wall was preserved, here the construction of the house is treated roughly with the intention of creating harmony between environment and man-made structure. Furthermore, the concept addressed the potential for shortcomings in detailing during construction.

Seeking perfection in roughness, Kuma eventually chose Chinese bamboo for the building's exterior, using it to layer over the façade rather than as structural support. He extols its qualities in terms of its appropriate raw delicacy. He refers to the

bamboo scaffold systems used on Chinese construction sites, and contrasts their delicacy and technical detail with those found in Japan. Screens of bamboo veil the outer walls of the Bamboo House and the ceilings, modulating the light and creating glimpsed views.

In plan the house is organized around a central meditative open space. The space contains a water feature and a tearoom enclosed in bamboo. This energizing core is visible from other areas of the house, and it separates the public and private spaces to either side. The structure's form is regarded by Kuma as an exchange of culture and

technology and an opportunity to establish a common perception of delicacy as a new method of communication.

Above
The top-floor plan reveals how the house is designed around a central open space.

The bamboo-fringed villa harmoniously blends the man-made with nature.

Below
The living room and terrace enjoy open views of the stark landscape.

Opposite
The central void, lined in bamboo and featuring a shallow pool, establishes a sense of calm over the house.

BAOAN RESIDENTIAL DEVELOPMENT, SHENZHEN

T.R. HAMZAH & YEANG, 2003–07

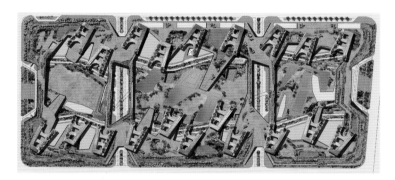

Covering a site of almost 18.4 hectares and designed for the Shean Yea Group, the Baoan development is predominantly residential (45,000 square metres), but also integrates retail, educational and recreation space. A central park with the apartment blocks clustered around it provides a focus for cultural activities, while a raised vehicle-free circulation ring creates a landscaped and pedestrian-friendly park setting.

The residential towers are generously spaced and orientated to maximize panoramic views of the park and waterfront. By mounding the periphery of the development, a seamless ground plane is created, encouraging pedestrian movement. It also produces a continuous landscape from street level up to the undersides of the towers, with continuing seams of vegetation that assist species migration, with the aim of nurturing a healthy ecosystem. In addition, sky-terraces reinvent the landscaped ground condition at higher levels, bringing inhabitants closer to their natural surroundings.

The towers are angled to minimize solar exposure during the summer. Sun-shading devices on alternate floors help to reduce solar penetration and provide internal comfort levels with low energy consumption during the summer. Walls throughout the apartment towers can be opened to allow through-ventilation. Conversely, they can be shut in winter to reduce heat loss. They can be controlled manually or mechanically, using photovoltaic cells.

A multiple landscape strategy forms the backbone to the development, creating an experiential journey for residents through a sequence of gardens. The development is entered from a tree-lined road to the carpark at level one. Residents then walk to the main lobby, which is defined by a central landscaped courtyard. Leaving the elevator at level two brings them on to the continuous vehicle-free landscaped ring. The swimming pool is located in the central park, a densely planted zone within the development. Landscaped pathways and garden terraces link the lift lobbies to the apartments, where landscaped courtyards look out over the parkland below.

Opposite
The staggered profile of the apartment blocks encourages natural cross-ventilation.

A series of landscaped settings creates a continuous journey through nature.

Above
The site plan and a perspective view reveal the openness of the architecture and the complexity of the landscape strategy.

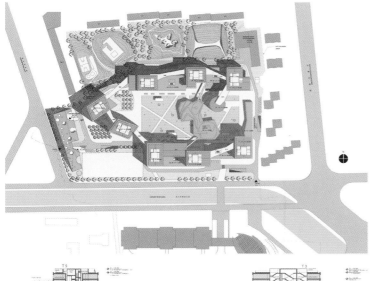

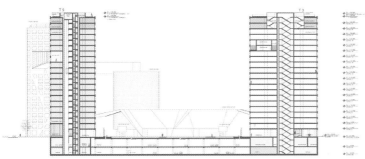

BEIJING HYBRID HOUSING, BEIJING

STEVEN HOLL ARCHITECTS, 2004–06

On a 6.18-hectare site adjacent to Beijing's old city wall, the developer, Modern Hongyun Real Estate Development, aspires to construct an ultra-modern model of twenty-first-century ecological urban living. With a total building area of 210,000 square metres, the programme encompasses 720 residential units, a cinema, kindergarten, galleries, shops, gym, café and 1000 underground parking spaces.

The intention of Steven Holl Architects is to avoid repeating Beijing's dominant tendency to produce 'object buildings'. The project, implemented in association with Beijing Capital Engineering Architecture Design, is imagined as a 'city within a city', where urban space is the central component, along with all the activities that are necessary to support the daily life of the projected 2500 inhabitants.

The polychrome architecture of ancient China inspires a new phenomenon: at night the undersides of the cantilevered parts of the development form glowing coloured membranes. Misting fountains from the water-retention basin activate the light at night in colourful clouds, while the floating Cineplex centrepiece has partial images of the films being played projected on its undersides and reflected in the water.

The design relates to the user's movements through space – the towers are organized in a particular rhythm so that as one travels through the site either horizontally or vertically, the views constantly change.

Eight towers are linked at the twentieth floor by a ring of cafés and services. Programmatically, this loop aspires to be semi-lattice-like rather than simply linear. It is hoped that the sky-loop and the base-loop will constantly generate random relationships, just as a modern city does.

The apartments are designed to accommodate hundreds of different layouts and typologies, emphasizing the concept of individuality as an urban lifestyle. The computer-designed prefabricated external structure of the eight towers allows for beam-free ceilings. Every apartment has two exposures with no interior hallways. Principles of feng shui are followed throughout the complex, which aims to achieve the US Green Building Council's sustainability rating.

The landscape concept is that of a 'garden of mounds'. Reusing the earth excavated for the new construction, five landscape mounds are formed, each fused with particular recreational facilities to suit different interests and groups of people. The new park is a semi-public space but use of the integrated functions is electronically controlled by residents' cards.

Opposite
The latticed forms of the towers form a loop around a central landscape.

Above
The site plan and a section and perspective reveal the embracing configuration of the residential towers in relation to the floating, cylindrical Cineplex and commercial amenities.

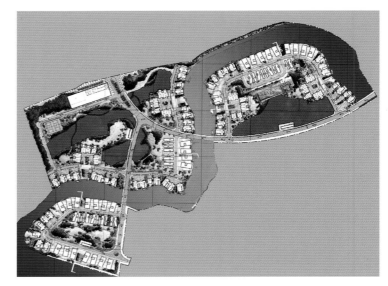

BOAO CANAL VILLAGE, HAINAN ISLAND

ROCCO YIM AND SEUNG H-SANG, 2001–02

This 188,220-square-metre project features 115 villas distributed along a series of canals in the semi-tropical seclusion of China's resort island of Hainan. Built for the pioneering Chinese developer Soho China, the waterside villas are interspersed with several tracts of primeval coconut groves, part of the natural beauty of the site.

Designed by Hong Kong architect Rocco Yim in association with Korean architect Seung H-Sang, IROJE Architects and Planners, the cuboid buildings range from two to four storeys. The serene ambience and intimate atmosphere of the place create an approach to hospitality very different from that of a standard five-star hotel. The villas have become popular with companies seeking settings for product launches, and they provide a relaxed atmosphere for corporate events, seminars and meetings. An additional asset is the adjacent Boao Golf Country Club.

The houses are elevated 4 metres from the ground to guard against flooding. They are planned around a central internal courtyard that distributes various living spaces with layouts that allow for multiple functions. The dwellings conform to several model types. Three-, four- and five-bedroom units are designed as garden villas, canal villas with integrated timber decks and mini dock, and river-view villas that face the Wanquan River.

Taking account of the local climate, the properties and courtyards are orientated to promote natural ventilation and shading. Generous terraces attached to the front and rear of the villas are not enclosed, so the views and cooling breezes can be fully appreciated.

At a broader scale, the units are clustered around open spaces that feed into the riverbank square and provide shared outdoor amenities.

The village is structured by a main road and small paths. The former allows access to all parts of the island, while the narrow paths within the village are solely for accessing the residences. The villas' club facilities are placed on the main arterial road, while docks and parking lots are conveniently connected so that, if they prefer, guests can reach their villa by boat.

Right
The masterplan outlines the residential buildings and associated landscapes.

An intricate palette of building and landscaping materials, as well as bamboo groves, helps to define the edges between the villas.

Open-plan interiors are flexible and multifunctional.

Opposite
Canal-facing villas are closely connected to the waterways.

Groups of houses nestle around shared courtyards that open to the waterfront.

CANNES GARDEN, TIAN HE, GUANGZHOU

RMJM HK, 2003–05

The two-phase masterplan for this residential development encompasses a 23-hectare site in the eastern suburbs of Guangzhou. When completed, it will comprise 109 residential towers ranging in height from six to eighteen floors. The development will be integrated with community facilities, including a clubhouse and two schools, and various retail amenities.

RMJM's approach to the first phase of the masterplan was intended to maintain a sense of community living, emphasizing the importance of the public realm in creating a sense of place and identity. Because of the size of the scheme, the priority was to devise a way to make spaces that work at a human scale. Dynamic clusters of self-contained outdoor areas are conceived as communal spaces that will foster community interaction and a sense of belonging. The apartment towers and clubhouse form a crescent that radiates out to connect visually with the adjacent stadium, helping to create a link between the green public spaces.

The architects' strategy for the phase-two masterplan was to reinforce the strong relationship between the 'architectural ribbons' and the communal spaces that surround them. This was achieved by putting greater emphasis on the continuity between groups of residential buildings and public areas. As a result, groups of independent but continuous contained spaces are established. These clusters are distinctive forms that nevertheless complement the neighbouring phase-one development.

Each cluster of buildings has an individually tailored landscape around it. The themes of spring, summer, autumn and winter provide a base around which the four landscaped spines are themed. Additional elements such as water features and pavilions are intended to create the sense of romance and refinement that typifies southern European cities. Meandering paths run through the site, creating lively outdoor leisure spaces, enriching communal living and promoting a green environment that allows urban dwellers to feel closer to nature.

Right

The masterplan of phase one of the development shows its clusters of communal spaces and ribbons of landscape.

The clubhouse is one of the various communal facilities in the development.

Opposite

The masterplanning emphasizes closeness to nature, from the veranda of the clubhouse to the comprehensive leisure facilities and meandering paths through the landscapes.

CANTILEVER HOUSE, COMMUNE-BY-THE-WALL, BEIJING

ANTONIO OCHOA-PICCARDO, 2000–01

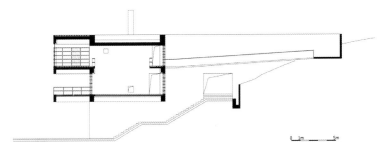

Perched on the rugged hills that flank the Great Wall with the valley folded around it, Cantilever House is conceived by the architect as a place that combines the history of human life and our current existence. In that respect he sees the house as an extension of man's alter ego, or his mirror image. Ochoa-Piccardo returns to the essential elements of shelter together with the possibility of transforming those fundamentals into habitable space and the memories that subsequently unfold.

Cantilever House results from the architect's study of the house as both nature and landscape. He explains this by defining the house as image, dwelling and refuge, a place in which we contemplate his universe and transform it. Yin and yang are successfully combined at different levels. The design originated as an experience of wintertime, and is therefore introverted and veiled in shadow (yin). However, in yang terms, it also openly relates to the landscape and embraces light.

Cantilevered out from the sloping terrain, the structure is highly conspicuous and provides cliff-hanging views. The architect plays off the exterior, which is hard-edged and muscular, against the inside, which is erotic, sensuous and warm – making the analogy of contrasting male and female.

The façade is patterned with openings and panels, allowing sunlight to flood the interior. The rust-coloured concrete takes its tone from the surrounding flora and rockscape, while barely touching it, enabling the landscape to flow freely underneath and around it. Formal entrance stairs ascend to an internal courtyard. Comparing the façades to a furniture-like system built of timber, Ochoa-Piccardo creates a random series of solids and voids that not only create visual pleasure but also designate particular functions. Private outdoor space is provided by a generous sheltered terrace. Further up, the roof garden distils the architect's vision of an ideal place of freedom, where the house becomes the landscape.

Top
A section through the cantilevered structure reveals its internal void.

Above
The sheltered terrace provides privacy and extensive views.

Left
The structure thrusts dramatically from the hillside.

Opposite
The verticality of the living spaces relates to the surrounding landscape.

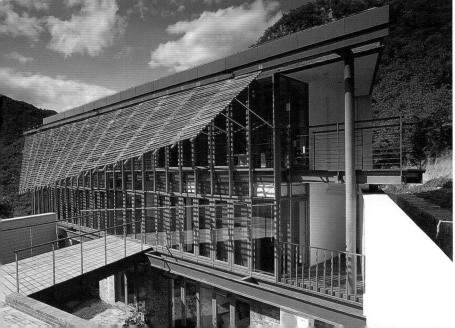

DISTORTED COURTYARD HOUSE, COMMUNE-BY-THE-WALL, BEIJING

ROCCO YIM, 2000–02

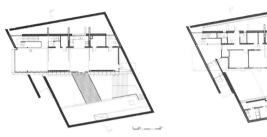

One of twelve resort chalets nestled in the foothills of the Shuiguan section of the Great Wall, the Distorted Courtyard House forms part of the Commune-By-The-Wall complex belonging to the developer Soho China. The site is conceived as a luxurious sanctuary to which well-heeled Beijingers can escape at weekends, its rural context providing complete respite from the fast pace of the city. Rocco Yim was among the fortunate few engaged to design one of the experimental showcase properties.

The two-storey Distorted Courtyard House is a study in the marriage of co-existing contrasts. The elevated light-filled living space is anchored to the ground by the fortress-like walls beneath it. While the upper, more public, functions are exposed to nature through floor-to-ceiling glass, the private domain is introverted, providing a solid buffer to the wilderness.

Old and new are also balanced in the combination of modern and traditional materials, the most obvious being the steel and glass of the upper box with the trellised bamboo curtain on the south-west elevation that diffuses natural light. Even the planning is an exercise in alignment and distortion. The double-height chalet is twisted, perched at an angle to the courtyard walls and minimizing the disturbance of the land.

The elevated communal zone also incorporates the master suite, which can be secluded by screen panels. Otherwise, the room does not dictate a specific use, leaving it open to guests to appropriate the space in whatever way they please. A service corridor lines one elevation, prompting a sequence of zones that ends with the communal open courtyard. The overriding experience is one of duality: the upper portion reaches out to the wilderness, at one with the outdoors, while the lower level answers people's need to feel protected.

Opposite
The solidity of the house's base contrasts with the transparency above, with its floor-to-ceiling windows screened from the glaring sun by a bamboo curtain.

Above
The upper- and lower-floor plans highlight the house's dual character, emphasized by the open views from the living area.

EMBASSY HOUSE, DONGZHIMEN, BEIJING

HOK INTERNATIONAL (ASIA/PACIFIC), 1997–2002

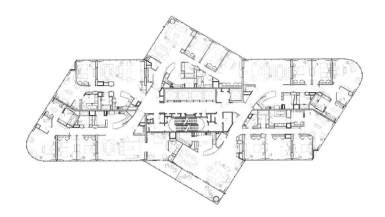

Embassy Hoouse offers luxury living quarters in the heart of Beijing's diplomatic area. The building's profile is prominent on the city skyline. Its streamlined modern form is unorthodox in terms of high-end residential towers, but its prestigious location, north of Dongzhimenwai Avenue between the Second and Third Ring Roads in Beijing's Second Embassy District, demanded an unusual approach.

HOK International (Asia/Pacific) was asked to design an upscale housing development that has more than a passing resemblance to a five-star international hotel. The project meets the expectations of a quality-conscious, primarily expatriate residential market, particularly diplomats from the neighbouring embassies. Leisure facilities are extensive, from the library and residents' bar, café and convenience shopping, to the well-equipped fitness complex. The last encompasses pool, sauna, steam, massage and jacuzzi facilities.

As might be anticipated, the architecture gives an impression of

international flair, from its glassy, fluid exterior to the blend of Chinese and Western features that characterize the 174 residential units, ranging from 213 to 274 square metres. A typical floor accommodates six two- and three-bedroom apartments, an arrangement that allows flexibility for future market needs. The top three floors contain four penthouse suites, each with four bedrooms. These give the summit of the building a subtle exterior architectural expression.

The orientation of the thirty-two-storey tower is designed to embrace its neighbours, the exterior completing a composition with the adjacent circular office building. The building's diagram is an overlay of two geometries. A skewed rectangular plan, smoothed off at its oblique corners, is intersected by a square, establishing a creative layout for planning the interior spaces. It provides each resident with the choice of south, east or west natural light.

Above
The skewed floor plan of the residential tower and detail of the elevation's articulation emphasize the building's creative layout.

Opposite
The shifted orientation of the tower is shown in relation to the highway and neighbouring buildings.

FATHER'S HOUSE, LANTIAN

MADA S.P.A.M., 1992–2003

This two-storey house was designed and built by MADA s.p.a.m.'s principal Qingyun Ma for his father. Sited in his homeland, a rolling valley in the rural enclave of Lantian, the context is rich in geomorphological features, the Jade Valley and Qingling mountain range forming a majestic backdrop that defines the whole territory. In the immediate vicinity of the house the landscape changes dramatically from steep mountain to gentle slopes and river valley, before flattening out into the infinitely expansive Middle Plateau.

The architect was inspired by the site of Father's House, an ambiguous position between the river, with its smooth water-polished stones, and the mountains, with their rocky outcrops.

The first and foremost concern of the design is the use of stone, both in terms of quantity and in employing local construction methodology. As the river works its way through the valley, rock falls supply abundant building material. Stone used in the house's construction was collected from the valley and transported up the hill by the architect's father and villagers. Where possible, local construction techniques and labour were used, which explains the house's simplified and homogeneous construction and appearance. The alien concrete is used as little as possible and is limited to the needs of distinct elements.

The treatment of the stone depends on where it occurs within the concrete frame. Locally, interior bamboo boards are typically used as formwork for concrete. Both stone and bamboo are common in the area, but in Father's House they are used in non-traditional applications to express a strong sense of modernity, while the materials and craftsmanship also reinforce an intensely local spirit. The principle also acknowledges the work of local peasants: during the winter months when there is no work in the fields, they make use of their building skills and experience.

Reflecting the rich diversity of the stone surfaces strewn across the landscape, the panels of the house similarly oscillate between different intensities of dark and light as well as rough and smooth textures. Folding doors of pressed bamboo board define the spaces between the interior and the exterior. The same material is continued on the inside where boards are treated with various colour varnishes to give their surfaces a monolithic finish.

Above
The varied rural context inspires the material quality of the house.

Below
The outdoor lap pool is ingeniously slotted between the house and the edge of the site.

Opposite
Stone used in the construction of the house was taken from the surrounding valley.

From the front courtyard of the house, its homogeneous and simple construction is evident.

FURNITURE HOUSE, COMMUNE-BY-THE-WALL, BEIJING

SHIGERU BAN, 2000–02

This modest 333-square-metre house stands in the undulating hills across which runs the Great Wall. Commissioned by the pioneering developer Redstone Industrie, Furniture House is one of twelve individually designed modern villas commissioned from a string of prominent Asian architects. Shigeru Ban's design has the effortless simplicity that can be achieved by an architect who enjoys the fundamental characteristics of materials and the way they are used.

The square plan frames an open inner square courtyard with a gateway at one end forming the main entrance. All the domestic spaces are accessed from an inner circulation passage that lines the courtyard, ensuring privacy from the outside world while offering intimacy with nature. The outer façade is punctuated with narrow floor-to-ceiling openings, except for the elevation accommodating the front entrance, which, other than six small square openings, is completely enclosed.

The primary living area is at the opposite end from the entrance, opening both to the courtyard and the rugged hills. Importance is attached to the space through its curved ceiling that arches over the otherwise exaggerated horizontality of the single-storey building.

Laminated bamboo plywood is the dominant structural component; however, its load-supporting function is combined with the interior demands of furniture – including bookshelves and storage cupboards – blurring the conventional distinction between structure and interior. The material is commonly used in China for concrete formwork, but here Ban explores the possibilities of its use as a building component. By laminating it with a specific glue within a controlled environment, he discovered that a strong material could be fabricated from bamboo strips. Tests conducted in Japan showed that this composite bamboo had a structural strength somewhere between those of steel and timber.

The house's remote location and limited budget had a major influence on the design and construction processes. Ban had the material prefabricated into a modular building system.

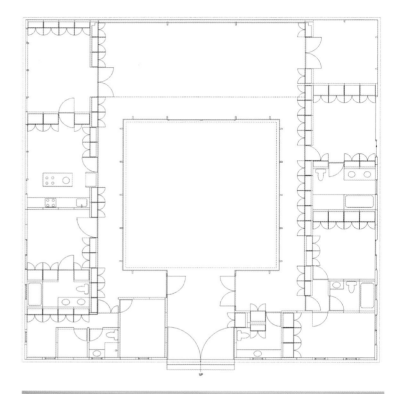

Right
The square floor plan outlines an inner courtyard that is open to the sky.

The main living space opens both to the hillside views and to the courtyard.

Opposite
The inner terrace creates different perspectives on each of the domestic spaces.

The distinctive horizontal form is broken by the gently arched roof of the living area.

JIANWAI SOHO, CHAOYANG, BEIJING

RIKEN YAMAMOTO, 2000–06

Prominent from Beijing's Third Ring Road, this partially constructed housing development occupies a prime location opposite the China World Trade Centre. It was masterminded by the Chinese developer Beijing Redstone Jianwai Real Estate, under its Soho China umbrella. The company conceives Jianwai Soho as a new-generation living and commercial environment, and the development follows the pioneering success of Soho China's first residential complex, Soho New Town, located a few blocks away.

Japanese architect Riken Yamamoto won the commission to design Jianwai Soho following an invited international competition managed by the developer. The site has a gross floor area of 700,000 square metres and will contain eighteen Soho apartment blocks accommodating 2069 residential units, two office buildings with up to 364 office spaces, and four villas. Commercial activities will include 400 retail stores, and cafés, restaurants and entertainment venues. Phase one of the construction programme, encompassing nine towers, was completed in April 2004.

The extraordinary cluster of towers is configured around a complex landscaped plateau of narrow winding lanes and grass-lined walkways, so that at ground level the experience of the streetscape recalls the scale and ambience of Beijing's traditional *hutongs*. But it is also intended to recreate the vibrancy and diversity that characterize the Western experience of Soho in New York or London. The architect has inserted fourteen alleyways that weave their way through the site and tie different parts of the community together. These meandering paths break into casual seating areas, gardens and play spaces. They also form the major arterial access points into the development, knitting it into the surrounding urban fabric.

By day or night, the strongly gridded elevations form an easily identifiable profile against the city skyline. Within the residential units, that language translates into living spaces that congregate around light-filled terraces with roof gardens. The regular configuration of the floor plans ensures that space is optimized while maintaining maximum flexibility.

Right
Floor-to-ceiling windows and expansive terraces allow natural light to penetrate the living spaces of the residential units.

Opposite
At street level, small-scale commercial activities permeate the apartment complex and occupy an internal circulation route of landscaped bridges and paths.

The gridded façades are illuminated at night.

SEE AND SEEN HOUSE, COMMUNE-BY-THE-WALL, BEIJING

CUI KAI, 2000–02

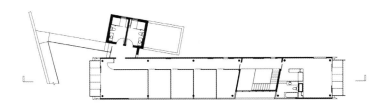

The principle of applying a concept to any number of sites where the terrain has various height differences was one of the initial ideas that Cui Kai explored with the design of See and Seen House. The architecture allows for 'repetition with diversity': the angle between the bedrooms and living room can be adjusted, glass treatments can be altered, bedroom compartments are flexible, and fixtures and interior materials can be varied.

The two-storey, 410-square-metre house capitalizes on the scenic vistas to the north and north-east of the site, while care is taken to avoid obstructing views from some of the other villas within the Commune-By-The-Wall complex – hence the villa's name. The living and dining areas are orientated to the north but are built on a sunken terrace that nestles in a thicket of trees and is covered with soil and planting to reduce its impact. The bedrooms are left exposed to the north-east and are raised on stilts, conforming to the flow of the topography while enjoying open views of the distant hills.

Without knowing exactly what kind of guests will make use of the villa, or what their relationships are (family, friends, colleagues *etc.*), Cui Kai has connected the living and dining areas to facilitate flexibility for gatherings. Similarly, the bedrooms can be separated into smaller or larger units to suit the habits of different groups of guests. Even the bathrooms can be segregated for male and female users. The master suite is given special treatment, raised above the terrace to access uninterrupted views and provide privacy.

A string of glowing lanterns illuminates the path to the villa at night. Warm light radiates from the glass entry hall, while light from the living areas spills on to the courtyard. Guests can congregate round the open kitchen, which is designed as a sociable space, like a bar. A separate service entrance connects the kitchen to the dining area so that food can be served at large parties without disturbing guests.

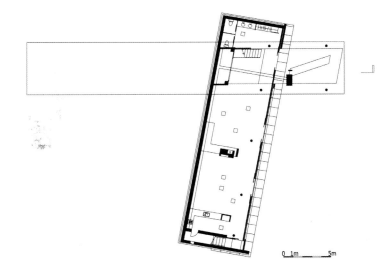

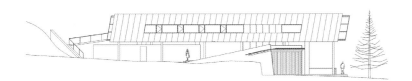

Right
Variations in floor plans show the intersecting volumes, which can be twisted and tilted to conform to the slope of the land.

Opposite
The exterior view conveys the clear definition of upper and lower volumes.

Floor-to-ceiling windows in the living and dining areas create close connections with the rural surroundings.

SHARED HOUSE, COMMUNE-BY-THE-WALL, BEIJING

KANIKA R'KUL, 2000–02

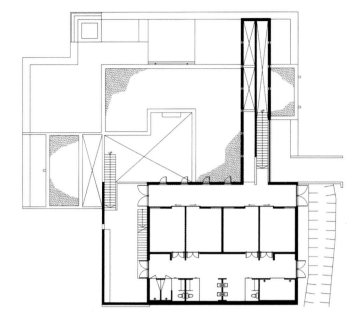

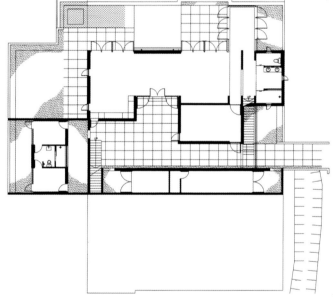

Focusing on the work-orientated lifestyle of users and their desire for a weekend home in the mountains, Kanika R'kul sees the Shared House as a place for family and friends. Aside from the representation of status and wealth, she regards time spent here as an opportunity for healing or simply returning to nature to regain a sense of balance.

The concept of sharing is apparent in the 524-square-metre house's ability to forge connections. Those between inside and outside and between people and nature are created with terraces, courts and roof decks. Interaction between occupants is tackled by emphasizing the importance of communal spaces such as living and dining areas in contrast to the privacy of upper-floor bedrooms. A more experimental approach to conventional domestic relationships is taken with the bathrooms, which confront traditional notions of public versus private.

The stark symbolism of the site, both physically challenging and visually inspiring,

is addressed through the scale, form, orientation and placing of openings. From every space in the house aspects of the site are revealed in various perspectives and at various scales. Intersecting volumes are visually related to each other by the exaggerated verticality of their window openings.

Experiencing the house requires patience in order fully to appreciate its configuration. It is approached as sequences of spaces that are not intended to be understood instantly. Each space offers an encounter between the man-made environment and nature in varying degrees of openness. These engagements extend from the quietness of the entry court and the sky to the extension of dining, living, and sitting areas out to the main terrace and the valleys below. An exterior staircase in the courtyard accesses the roof, where the extreme openness of the deck reveals views of the mountain ranges in their entirety.

Right
Floor plans demonstrate how the villa explores different layers of complexity in the relationships between indoors and outdoors.

Bedrooms and bathrooms on the upper floor are separated by a communal hall.

Opposite
The intersecting volumes of the crisp white villa present a stark counterpoint to the rugged landscape.

SPLIT HOUSE, COMMUNE-BY-THE-WALL, BEIJING

YUNG HO CHANG, 2000–02

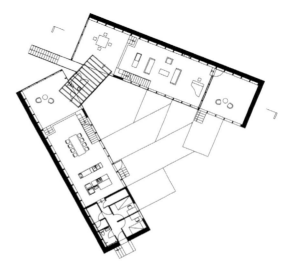

The two-storey wood-frame and compressed-earth structure occupies the furthest point of the Commune-By-The-Wall site, at the top of the valley. It earns its name from its split plan. The 449-square-metre volume is sliced down the middle, its ends pulled apart at a 45-degree angle. The process creates numerous different perspectives and experiences as one moves through the segmented spaces, while the intervening open area forms a courtyard that the architect describes as "half natural, half architectural".

The split format stems from the architect's understanding of the site: between the mountains and the rivers. With minimal disturbance to existing features, Yung Ho Chang preserves the path of a tiny creek as it flows under the house at the point where the two wings are closest. This part of the house is distinguished by a raised glass-floored bridge. It defines the entrance vestibule, drawing the outdoors in, and orientating the two mirrored wings of the house.

Conceived as a generic modular concept, the Split House is designed to adapt to the contours of any number of site conditions. By changing the angle between the two blocks, the house can alter its footprint in various ways: forming a single house or two parallel units, a long linear structure or a back-to-back composition.

Built in the Chinese tradition, with timber frame and clay walls, the Split House is an ecologically sound structure. Its impact on the environment is minimal, and its structure responds to the climate in a way that optimizes comfort for the inhabitants. The rammed-earth walls act as insulation, keeping the house warm in winter and cool in summer. The architect insists that, while the Split House represents a respect for tradition, it is not an attempt to recreate it; rather, it is an attempt to create a new architectural vision for a modern China.

Right
The uppper- and lower-floor plans define sleeping and living/dining areas respectively.

The view across the roofscape shows Split House encircled by mountains.

Opposite
The split format of the two wings creates a natural semi-open courtyard.

Dining and living spaces are highly insulated by rammed-earth walls.

STAFF RESIDENCE, DONGGUAN INSTITUTE OF TECHNOLOGY, SONGSHAN LAKE NEW TOWN, DONGGUAN, GUANGDONG

ATELIER ZHANGLEI, 2002–04 (PHASE ONE)

Living quarters for teachers and staff at the Dongguan Institute of Technology are provided by an apartment building, row houses, and a dormitory for single teaching staff. The confined site is characterized by undulating hills, and the three building components are delineated by the topography. While each has its own characteristics in terms of use and identity, together they interact, forming a village-like settlement on the campus. Linked by winding streets that divide the site naturally from east to west, the former is designated for the dormitory, while the apartments and row houses occupy the latter.

The first phase of the dormitory development comprises more than 200 rooms with private bathrooms. Although climate is not as significant a concern here as it is in other parts of China, ventilation and protection from sunlight are considered in the development's spatial organization. An 8-metre height difference between the sides of the building was integrated in the design by establishing a bicycle-parking lot on the ground floor and making some structural adjustments to the sixth and fourth floors, reducing earthworks by making use of the existing terrain. Inner courtyards play an important role in improving the living environment, as well as enabling various outdoor activities.

In the apartment building, each household is allocated 150 square metres and a two-storey volume. Bathroom and kitchen are fixed, but other features, such as the number of bedrooms and balcony placement, can be adapted to suit different users. With bedrooms and living space being the principal variables between one household and another, these active elements are allocated to the southern façade. By contrast, the northern elevation is relatively fixed. The location and size of windows correspond to the use of each room, which explains the difference between the south and north elevations.

A more generous index of 180 square metres applies to the two-storey row houses. The two terraced blocks running from east to west are planned along the river. Each house has a front and back courtyard and, because they lie on lower ground, they do not obstruct views from the dormitory quarters behind.

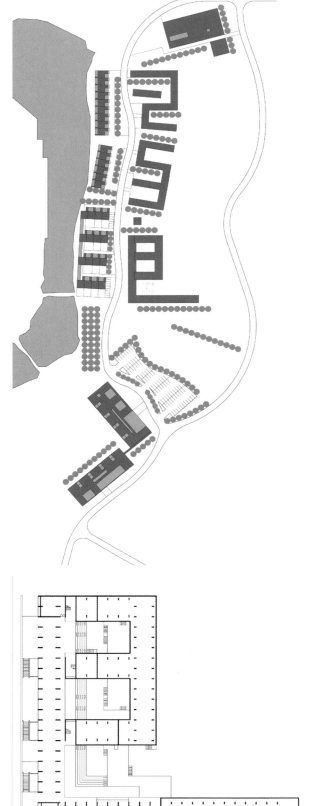

Right
The site plan is constrained by various geographical features.

The dormitory building is planned around a series of inner courtyards.

Opposite
The row houses are clustered along the river, while the varied elevations of the apartment block indicate the fixed and flexible elements of individual units.

STUDIO HOUSE, BEIJING

FAKE DESIGN, 1999–2000

This stand-alone 500-square-metre house designed as an artist's studio was tailor-made for its owner, Ai Weiwei. It has a reinforced skeleton frame structure, which has been left exposed on its inner surfaces with red-brick infill panels.

The monolithic exterior of the building communicates very little in terms of its function. Grey facing brick forms a sombre outer skin. Window openings are not abundant, the few openings there are being strategically placed according to the particular function accommodated inside.

The principal planning of the two-storey house combines a double-height studio set at a right-angle to the domestic realm. The fully enclosed studio is only accessible from the house, its solid encasement providing security and protection while creating an introverted environment. Its only sources of light are two slot skylights.

The residential domain is wrapped around one end of the studio. The two entities, one plugged into the other, create an intimate bond, their boundaries subtly giving way and overlapping on both levels. The living room is also double-height and

occupies one end of the linear domestic unit. The remaining functions follow sequentially, but a staircase to an upper gallery reinforces the connection between both domains and enhances the verticality of the architecture.

The materials used seem to refer to traditional Chinese houses. Their number is kept to a minimum, evoking an ascetic quality that is serene and meditative, and presumably conducive to creativity. Shafts of light streak the interior in places that the owner finds important, and add to the house's fortress-like character.

Above
The monolithic exterior of the studio and residence conceals the close connections between the two.

Below
The verticality of space is explored in the studio and living area, as well as the upstairs gallery.

Opposite
Light is very tightly controlled, filtering into spaces such as the living room and upstairs bathroom through clearly defined openings.

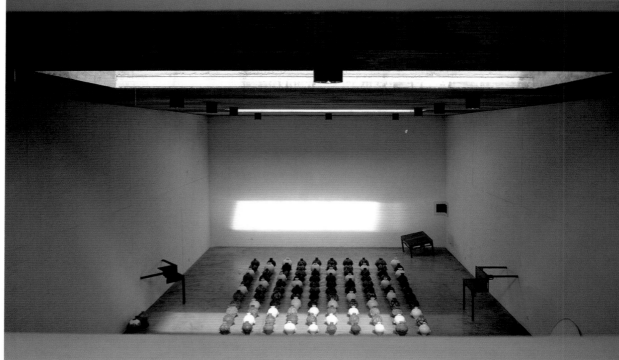

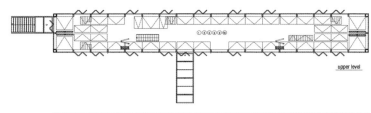
upper level

middle level

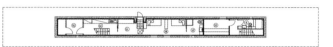
lower level

SUITCASE HOUSE, COMMUNE-BY-THE-WALL, BEIJING

GARY CHANG, 2000–02

In a sheltered valley at the foot of the Great Wall at Badaling Shuiguan outside Beijing, twelve freestanding structures form the first phase of the Commune-By-The-Wall hotel complex conceived by the entrepreneurial Soho China developer team. Talented young Asian architects have been invited to create a collection of experimental properties. The Suitcase House, designed by Gary Chang, founder and director of Edge Design Institute, challenges the conventional notion of a home, attempting to rethink the nature of intimacy, privacy, spontaneity and flexibility. The architecture aims to create the ultimate in adaptability so that infinite domestic, and other, scenarios become possible.

A north–south orientation makes the most of views of the Great Wall and solar exposure. The dwelling is vertically stacked in layers. Although non-hierarchical in its unoccupied form, the space becomes alive by reacting to the specifics of its inhabitants – type of activity, number of guests, degrees of privacy and enclosure, and so on. The space transforms itself with the help of mobile elements integrated with the architecture. A single volume metamorphoses into a sequence of rooms, and concealed amenities reveal themselves, differentiating the spaces.

These hidden functions are contained in the bottom stratum of the building. Pneumatically hinged floor doors flip up to provide functional elements that also form their own chambers. Besides the basics of bedroom, bathroom, kitchen and storage, there are more indulgent environments, including a music room, library, study, sauna, lounge and meditation chamber. The last has a glazed floor bringing nature into the space. A drop-down staircase in the ceiling of the main space allows access to the rooftop terrace with its unobstructed vista.

With all the sliding partitions in use, the Suitcase House becomes a long introverted space, 44 × 5 metres. As the day proceeds, different functions may appear and their needs are met. In the evening, entertaining is simple as the interior reinvents itself as an expansive lounge and dining salon. The building skin reflects this inner stratification. Full-height double-glazed folding doors form the outer wrapping, while the inner layers are a moving matrix of screens and panels. The façade is in constant flux, dictated by the movements of the occupants, and blurring the definitions of house, interior and furniture.

Opposite
Plans of the linear structure reveal its internal functional features.

The interior adapts itself to the needs of specific users by day and night.

Above and right
The north–south alignment of the house makes the most of views of the Great Wall.

The main living space rests above the ground, with supporting functions anchored below.

TRI-HOUSE, DIANSHANHU, KUNSHAN, JIANGSU

ATELIER DESHAUS, 2001–03

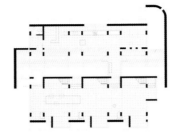

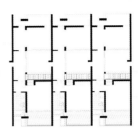

Situated in a country housing estate beside the Dianshan Lake, this residence was designed for three friends. The property was conceived as a weekend rural retreat using a minimalist language that instantly sets it apart from the surrounding developments, which are typically characterized by pitched roofs. For the clients, the overriding concern was to be able to live together here with their families. As partners, they also need to work together whenever they wish.

The two-storey structure consists of four cross walls and four longitudinal walls placed on a formal orthogonal grid. The ground floor contains the public studio, the kitchen and the dining room. However, the building earns its name from the upper floor, which accommodates three individual living units. The horizontal walls divide the vistas and restrict the view available from the open and flexible lower floor, while the vertical walls on the upper level lead the eye across the garden towards the lake.

Among the primary features of the residence are the courtyard spaces, which are inserted between rooms to allow sunlight into the north wings. Three small yards, separated on the second floor, form a single large area on the ground, where dozens of bamboos are planted in a linear strip at the side of the workshop. The bamboos are treated as important space elements, humanizing the scale of the yard and lending a poetic charm.

Although constructed in the form of pure cubes, in contrast to the mansard roofs of neighbouring buildings, the exterior walls of the house do bear similarities to the surrounding properties in terms of the facing stones and white-painted walls. The stonework is fixed on to the concrete walls like a skin, a construction method that is currently widely adopted in China. What distinguishes the walls is the edge treatment: the fixing is not disguised but explicitly revealed by exposing the details at the ends of the walls.

Square grey bricks are traditionally used for flooring and commonly used in the halls of ancient houses in this region, south of the Yangzi River. Here the bricks are used for the floors of all the rooms on the lower level, as well as the staircase and bathrooms. Their fine texture and subtle warmth also make them useful for cladding the bathroom walls and the surfaces of several pieces of simple furniture. In contrast, the bedrooms have bamboo floors.

Opposite
The two-storey structure is clearly defined both horizontally and vertically, providing privacy as well as shared space.

Above and right
The three-in-one villa is set in rural surroundings and uses materials that are typical of the area.

XINZHAO JIAYUAN RESIDENTIAL AREA, BEIJING

GMP – VON GERKAN, MARG UND PARTNER ARCHITECTS, 2000–04

Four large districts contain a total of 5800 apartments. The first construction phase, completed in 2002, produced 1468 new homes. The architects employed an axial grid system to divide the almost square masterplan into four. The central spine, which runs from north to south, contains the major activities and events, while a green park landscape is placed perpendicularly, stretching east to west.

Each neighbourhood is a linear structure with a parallel but staggered alignment. The rows of buildings configured east to west maximize the number of north–south-facing apartments. At intervals the linear framework is interrupted, allowing wider passages of open space to penetrate between the developments. This produces a series of courtyard spaces of various proportions, and the resulting hierarchy delineates the urban landscape by progressively dividing it from large to small scales. From terraced houses to high-rise towers, a wide choice of residential types accommodates different modes of living.

Both the green main axis and the smaller courtyards within each district provide opportunities for outdoor recreation and relaxation in close proximity to the apartments. All the residential units are orientated south towards an extensive green area, creating buildings that are equally attractive. The number of storeys also varies from one district to another according to the location of the buildings.

The residential towers accentuate the curved southern edge of the surrounding parkland, and present a contrast with the rectilinear structures. While the boundaries of each district are enclosed on all sides, along the main roads the development follows the street pattern, forming a spatial edge for future public streetscapes. However, the axial grid penetrates the roadside developments and connects to the public amenities, such as the shopping centre in the south-east and other commercial uses along the axis.

The circulation is carefully considered, enabling the central boulevard and the 'park drive' running south of the tower blocks to interconnect all the districts in a loop. There are plans for a continuous pedestrian network comprising roadside pavements and separate pathways. Paved footpaths also cross the green courtyards from north to south, joining the passageways within the rows of blocks.

Opposite
The residential blocks are orientated around landscaped courtyards.

Left
The masterplan is driven by the juxtaposition of four residential districts. Its boundaries are clearly delineated and follow the street development.

SCHOOLS, COLLEGES AND LIBRARIES

CHINESE ACADEMY OF SCIENCE LIBRARY,
ZHONG GUANCUN, BEIJING
INSTITUTE OF ARCHITECTURE DESIGN & RESEARCH,
CHINESE ACADEMY OF SCIENCE

CHUANGYE MANSION, TSINGHUA SCIENCE AND
TECHNOLOGY CAMPUS, BEIJING
XWG (BEIJING TSINGHUA ARCHITECTURAL DESIGN & CONSULTATION)

DONGGUAN INSTITUTE OF TECHNOLOGY, SONGSHAN LAKE
NEW TOWN, DONGGUAN, GUANGDONG
ATELIER DESHAUS

GERMAN SCHOOL AND APARTMENT HOUSE,
LIANGMAQIAO LU, BEIJING
GMP – VON GERKAN, MARG UND PARTNER ARCHITECTS

NATIONAL ACCOUNTANCY INSTITUTE, SHUNYI TIANZHU
DEVELOPMENT ZONE, BEIJING
JINAO KANN FINCH DESIGN GROUP

NATIONAL LIBRARY OF CHINA, BEIJING
KSP ENGEL UND ZIMMERMANN ARCHITECTS

SHENZHEN UNIVERSITY TOWN ADMINISTRATIVE CENTRE
AND LIBRARY, SHENZHEN
RMJM HK

SICHUAN FINE ARTS INSTITUTE, CHONGQING
JIAKUN ARCHITECTS

SONGYUE KINDERGARTEN, XIAMEN, FUJIAN
LUO SIWEI

TEACHING BUILDING, GRADUATE DEPARTMENT,
CHINESE ACADEMY OF SCIENCE, ZHONG GUANCUN, BEIJING
INSTITUTE OF ARCHITECTURE DESIGN & RESEARCH,
CHINESE ACADEMY OF SCIENCE

TIANJIN TAIDA PRIMARY SCHOOL, TIANJIN
CHINA ARCHITECTURE DESIGN & RESEARCH GROUP

WENZHENG COLLEGE LIBRARY, SUZHOU UNIVERSITY,
YUE XI, WU XIAN, SUZHOU
AMATEUR ARCHITECTURE STUDIO

YANCHENG MEDICAL SCHOOL LIBRARY, YANCHENG, JIANGSU
ZHU JINGXIANG STUDIO

YANCHENG YOUTH CENTRE, YANCHENG, JIANGSU
ZHU JINGXIANG STUDIO

CHINESE ACADEMY OF SCIENCE LIBRARY, ZHONG GUANCUN, BEIJING

INSTITUTE OF ARCHITECTURE DESIGN & RESEARCH, CHINESE ACADEMY OF SCIENCE, 1999–2002

This much-praised development occupies a prominent position at the heart of the Chinese Academy of Science's campus, and plays a significant symbolic role in projecting the academy's image.

The architects have formulated the building as an entity that can only be fully appreciated when it is experienced. The layering of spaces introduces multiple perspectives as one moves through the complex. The architects also conceive the building as a container, implying that it has a specific functional role but also that it has a universal quality.

Traditional Western methods of stone- and bricklaying are used alongside authentic Chinese timber construction. The process of building wood structures has evolved dramatically in China and has

now reached a highly advanced level that is technologically driven, encouraging sophisticated new forms of modern architecture to emerge. This library is a timely example. Where possible, the architecture is open, providing vistas of what lies beyond.

The building conveys grandeur as well as sublimity, its formal entrance with a majestic gateway and regal staircase giving way to subtleties that await discovery. The main courtyard forms the central focus, opening to the south-west to take advantage of the prevailing breezes and the views. Designed like a cultural palace or an important place of learning, it is here that the richness of space can be explored and where the architects reveal the events hidden inside.

Right
An interior view highlights the layering of spaces.

Opposite
The library building is surrounded by open parkland. From the staircase entrance there are vistas through to and beyond the internal courtyard.

CHUANGYE MANSION, TSINGHUA SCIENCE AND TECHNOLOGY CAMPUS, BEIJING

XWG (BEIJING TSINGHUA ARCHITECTURAL DESIGN & CONSULTATION), 2001–03

Architecturally, Chuangye Mansion is conceived as a container of different exploratory ideas from the fields of consciousness and cognition. These ideas are influenced by the experience of the site and its peripheral context. The resulting form encompasses all these parameters. XWG explored the structural relationship between a container and its contents as a constantly changing dynamic, comparing its character to that of a fish swimming in a glass aquarium.

The basic tone of the site is fixed by the surrounding rectilinear office buildings, neighbouring blocks and residential areas. There is also a well-organized transport network that provides a structured clarity to the campus. Chuangye Mansion evolved in a similar manner.

To the east, the site borders the central green landscape of the Tsinghua Science Park building complex, whose focal position and attractive setting determined the transparent east volume of the building. A viewing terrace inserted on floors eight and nine and a 'floating' window wall from floors ten to twelve capitalize on the open views.

The landscape to the west includes picturesque features such as the West Mountain and Jade Spring Mountain, which can be seen from the seventh floor upwards. They form a dramatic backdrop to the Weiming Lake and the Tower of the Fragrance of the Buddha. The concavity of the west side of the building means that users can enjoy the views without the glare of the setting sun in summer.

Its owner envisioned Chuangye Mansion – an incubator of ideas – as a metaphor for 'mother' and 'new-born'. The 'new-born' idea inspired the wing building to the south. The neighbouring angular high-rise towers, and the general plan of the park, inspired the idea of recessing the south wing, reflecting the profile of the undulating mountains.

The Science Park is adjacent to the campus of Tsinghua University, whose architectural style features the grey brick wall of its earliest building, Tsinghua Xuetang, built in 1909. Grey therefore provides the basic palette, underlining the original architectural spirit of Tsinghua.

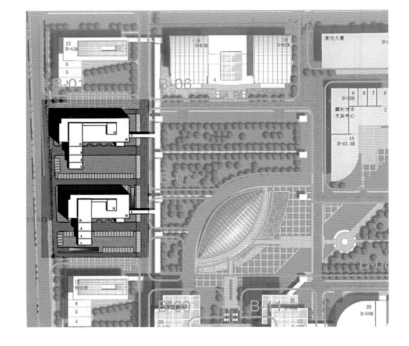

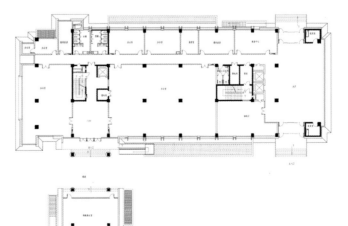

Right
The site plan shows the location of Chuangye Mansion in relation to the other buildings on the campus.

Ground-floor plan of the two wings.

Opposite
The articulation of the façade is a direct response to the building's outlook towards both the mountains and the Science Park building complex.

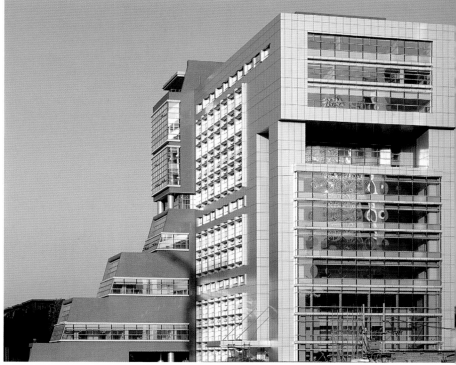

DONGGUAN INSTITUTE OF TECHNOLOGY, SONGSHAN LAKE NEW TOWN, DONGGUAN, GUANGDONG

ATELIER DESHAUS, 2002–04

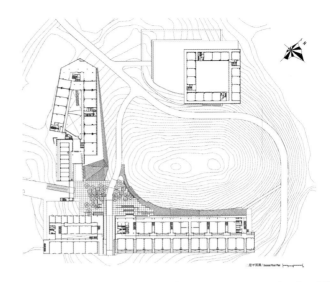

The Dongguan Institute of Technology is sited in the undulating hills of the Songshan Lake New Town. Litchi trees cover the landscape, while the valleys form natural ponds. The three buildings – for the electrical engineering, computer science and liberal arts departments – nestle around a hill that rises about 20 metres. The north-east side of the site, facing a pond, is kept open, minimizing disturbance to the landscape and preserving the extended views. The architects applied a rational methodology to creating an appropriate campus atmosphere for the three academic buildings, while the buildings' varied scales and orientation produce a range of relationships with the topography.

The linear Electrical Engineering Department Building is aligned along the contours of the south-east side of the hill. Because of its large size, it adopts a horizontal posture, which is juxtaposed with the undulating hills. The two distinct but coexisting forms are brought into sharp contrast. Along the slope, several passages and stairways are cut through the building, recalling the experience of climbing the surrounding hills. Internally, the circulation corridors alternate with open spaces, introducing scenic views from the other side. Glass channels on either side of the penetrated spaces filter the natural scenery into the building, establishing an intimate relationship with the landscape.

The elevated Liberal Arts Department Building, with its square courtyard, is sited on the north-west edge of the hill. The first floor is partially buried, merging into the landscape. Because of changes in the ground level, two sides of the first floor remain open, offering views towards the pond. The rest of the floor receives sunlight through an L-shaped internal courtyard. The first-floor roof forms an open terrace, while the square upper floors are elevated above the terrace. The combination of courtyard, arcade and terrace create a focused public open space.

Finally, the Computer Science Department Building is sited on the south-west side of the hill. Its zigzag form cradles a small internal courtyard, which lies parallel to the school's Main Academic Building across the valley. To gain sufficient daylight, the surrounding slopes were partially cut away and supported by retaining walls. The corridors on the first two floors are open to the internal courtyard, while those on the third and fourth floors face outwards, meeting at the north end like two streets leading up to a plaza or the two side frames of a boat coming together at the foredeck. A straight flight of stairs connects the internal courtyard with the northern terrace on the third floor, tying the inside and outside corridors together.

Right
The site plan shows the three buildings nestled around a hill.

The internal corridors of the Electrical Engineering Department Building lead up to stunning views of the scenery.

Opposite
The elevated Liberal Arts Department Building encloses a square courtyard, while outward-facing colonnades relate to the natural landscape.

The inner courtyard of the Computer Science Department Building is shown at a more intimate scale.

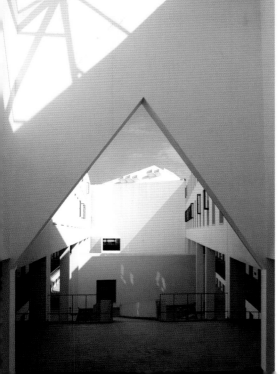

GERMAN SCHOOL AND APARTMENT HOUSE, LIANGMAQIAO LU, BEIJING

GMP – VON GERKAN, MARG UND PARTNER ARCHITECTS,

1998–2000

Situated in Beijing's Third Diplomatic District, a busy and varied neighbourhood, this project includes kindergarten facilities and a separate residential building for diplomats and their families. The context determined that the complex should have clearly defined edges delineating the site and strategically placed open spaces segregating different components of the project.

The architects have organized the clusters of buildings using an interplay of open spaces, accentuating delimitation and openness by reinterpreting the traditional Chinese approach of grouping building structures hierarchically. An ensemble is formed by emphasizing the school building horizontally, in contrast to the vertical residential quarters. Both functional components are ordered in a series of layers, generating a coherent overall structure.

The pair of three-storey school blocks flank a central building that accommodates the foyer, great hall and sports hall. These follow a progressive sequence of spaces with mobile partition walls. The fluidity this provides also enables the space to be used for functions other than school activities. A transparent circulation system is assisted by the formal ordering of the building units

and the application of different materials according to function. Parquet flooring and timber wall cladding provide a distinctive focus and a counterpoint to the white walls and red floors of the teaching areas. Elements such as doors, frames and furniture are made from aubergine-tinged concrete panels, normally used as shuttering boards for in-situ concrete construction.

Landscaped roof terraces provide open spaces that are integrated with the classroom wings on the upper floors. Their height gives protection from traffic noise and pollution, creating a green enclave for reading, leisure and open-air classes.

Orientated towards the east, the apartment block contains forty-five residential units with four or six on each floor and five different types ranging from 65 to 210 square metres of floor area. An open glass hall connects the two parallel nine-storey blocks, but the primary entrance is on the main road. A sheltered foyer provides access to the apartments by detached stairwells and lifts. Generous living spaces are further enlarged with winter gardens, and the yellow prefabricated-concrete façade and yellow flooring complement the imperial red school complex.

Right
The school block provides a central focus for the surrounding residential community.

Opposite
An interplay of open spaces feeds into the brick-coloured façade of the school building.

NATIONAL ACCOUNTANCY INSTITUTE, SHUNYI TIANZHU DEVELOPMENT ZONE, BEIJING

JINAO KANN FINCH DESIGN GROUP, 1998–2001

Located in the Shunyi Tianzhu Development Zone, the site is influenced by two major expressways that run diagonally in a north-east direction, one of them linking with the international airport. As the orientation of these highways goes against the grain of the city's old road grid, whose axis generally runs north to south, all the roads in the area are forced to turn through 45 degrees in either direction.

In planning the institute, the architects wanted to return the site to a north–south orientation, which provides a more natural setting for life in northern China. To avoid conflict with the overlapping road grids, the architects chose a geometric form, hence the large egg-shaped structure at the heart of the site. An education building placed to the south marks out the learning zone from the living quarters at the back.

A slope rising from north to south in front of the main building obstructs views of the carpark, so users enjoy vistas of pristine landscaped open space with lush greenery and treetops in the distance. A group of student dormitory blocks behind the main building is configured in a U, embracing an inner courtyard. The student canteen to the north looks on to this area at ground level. Together with the logistics building and gymnasium to the east, an urban street is created that encourages community interaction and identity. A man-made hill to the west falls away to a lake beyond, where the teaching staff apartments are located.

The simple oval form of the main building belies its complex programme: there are four lecture theatres at the two ends and a central four-storey atrium. The atrium is flanked by six teaching units, each separated either by a staircase, lift or rest platform. On the south façade, a ventilated triple-glazed curtain-wall system edges the teaching units, the energy-saving air void between the double and single layers of glass allowing ventilation in summer and heat storage in winter.

Above
An aerial view of the elliptical site demonstrates how its configuration creates a harmonious, self-contained form against the surrounding tangle of road systems.

Below
The transparency of the main building brings light and views into the teaching and circulation spaces.

Opposite
The main teaching building is elliptical in form. Its surrounding features adopt a similar geometry.

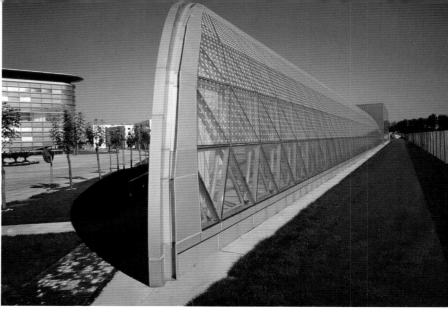

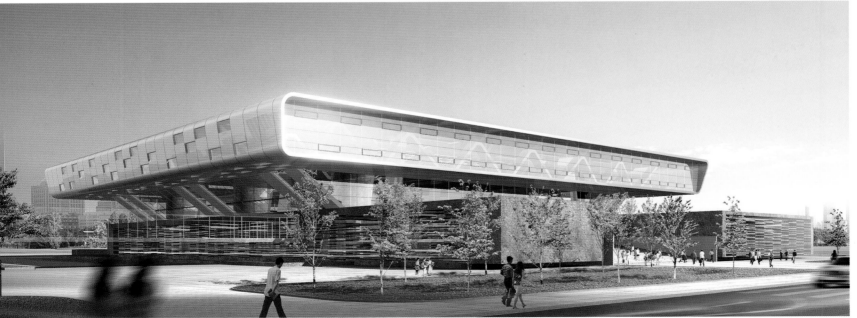

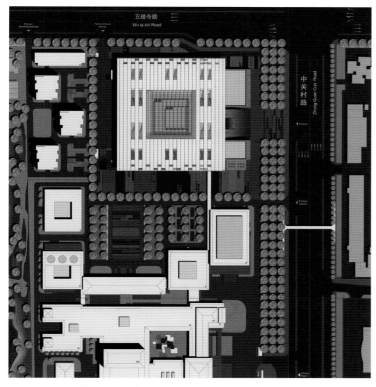

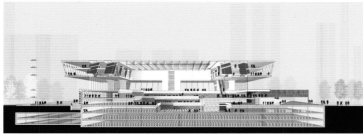

NATIONAL LIBRARY OF CHINA, BEIJING

KSP ENGEL UND ZIMMERMANN ARCHITECTS, 2003–07

Construction of the National Library of China began with a competition involving nine prominent practices from both China and overseas. The brief called for an extension to the existing library, which would expand its capacity by 77,000 square metres in order to accommodate approximately 12 million books and around 12,000 visitors daily.

One of the key future-orientated components of the project is the digital library. However, the Si Ku Quan Shu collection of manuscripts, written during the reign of Emperor Ch'ein Lung (1736–95) in the Ch'ing dynasty (1644–1912), and of enormous historical and cultural significance, will also be housed in the new building.

The architecture derives from this collection, which is confined to the basement structure. Inspired by the unearthing of archaeological layers of culture, the space circulates around several levels. The largest area contains the contemporary library with reading rooms, reference works and a reference library. Suspended over this is the digital library, a sign of the future. This symbolic linking of past, present and future is evident as interdependent, simultaneously merging elements.

The rectangular ensemble, measuring 90 × 119 metres, is horizontally organized and developed. From the front of the building the perspective appears smaller; the actual dimensions of the building only become evident from a higher vantage point. The library is surrounded by a formal garden, which further emphasizes the building's well-defined composition. The two upper storeys resemble a large book with gently rounded contours.

Visitors approach through the garden and a geometrically arranged grove at the entrance. From there, a broad staircase, flanked by two lower building sections, leads to the upper level, where there are sweeping views across the library and into the expansive steel structure spanning the roof. The frame rests on just six points, leaving the floor relatively open. Different levels are woven into each other with rows of bookshelves alternating with reading areas.

On the top floor, visitors can look into the digital library with its enormous, clearly structured plan. From here, there are also exterior views through the glass rear wall. Daylight permeates the inner spaces; the introverted, enclosed focus typical of conventional libraries is avoided. Even in the library's core, the glazed vault holding the Si Ku Quan Shu collection, bound in wooden panels, remains visible.

Opposite
The exaggerated horizontal form of the digital library is suspended over the contemporary and historical core underneath.

Left
The library sits in a formal garden setting.

A long section reveals the buried inner core of the library facility.

Light and open views characterize the inner spaces with minimal structural columns.

SHENZHEN UNIVERSITY TOWN ADMINISTRATIVE CENTRE AND LIBRARY, SHENZHEN

RMJM HK, 2004–07

Opposite
An aerial perspective of the education complex shows how its bridge connects the two principal functions.

At night the structure forms a soft, undulating profile against the river landscape.

Above
The masterplan indicates the separation of the facility's major uses.

Below
Materials and finishes are chosen to enhance the impact of internal architectural features.

A limited competition for the design of the Shenzhen University's library and administrative centre called for a 'gateway icon' for the new tripartite university campus formed by the Chin Hua, Harbin and Beijing Universities campus districts. RMJM's winning proposal incorporates a north–south axial pedestrian bridge that connects two principal banded segments of the site's masterplan. This allows the building to be highly accessible, yet independent.

The university town's 5.2-hectare site in the suburbs of Shenzhen is at the edge of a piece of hilly land that forms a stunning natural background. Over the winding Dasha River that cuts across the site, the bridge connects the two halves of the campus. Observing the concept of 'unity and modernity', the long, undulating form of RMJM's design draws its inspiration from the natural environment and echoes the gentle form of the surrounding hills, while the high-tech materials express the language of education and knowledge.

The project lies at the interface of the university campuses. While the entrance plaza, link bridge and roof garden provide a series of important public spaces for the entire campus, the building itself will become a cutting-edge landmark. Under an undulating roof it brings together the 6350-square-metre administrative centre and 29,150-square-metre library elements required by the three universities.

Many of the internal spaces are open plan. Full-height curtain walls along the east and west façades allow maximum daylight to penetrate the building while minimizing its visual mass within the campus.

The architecture focuses on the functionality and quality of the space and the rational use of materials. Glass, aluminium and steel were selected for the exterior because of their durability, low maintenance and the sense of modernity they express.

Sustainable measures are incorporated in the design. To reach the optimum balance between cost and function, different types of glazing – clear, reflective and low-e coated – were applied to different sides of the building. The 200-metre-long glass façade of the library has a solar coating and sun-shading devices to reduce solar gain. The brise-soleil is made of 800-mm-wide perforated aluminium panels.

SICHUAN FINE ARTS INSTITUTE, CHONGQING

JIAKUN ARCHITECTS, 2002–04

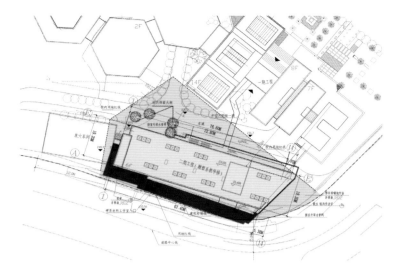

This project incorporates the teaching building of the Sichuan Fine Arts Institute's sculpture department, which occupies a confined corner of the campus. Its faceted profile, punctured by voids and terraces, suits its serious academic function without being obviously sculptural in form.

The subject being taught here meant that a large number of day-lit classrooms were needed. However, the volume specified exceeded the area that the building footprint allowed. This explains why the building protrudes outwards towards the top, within defined limits, in order to gain the largest-possible floor area.

The fourth and fifth levels of the building are made concave, creating two layers of outdoor space while also allowing daylight to penetrate classrooms on the third floor.

Chongqing's summers are stiflingly hot, and in response the architect has paid attention to the issue of natural ventilation, enhancing the flow of air through the classrooms of the teaching building. On the west and south elevations the lattice effect of a double-height tracery wall reduces the glare of the sun yet maintains the flow of ventilation across the wall.

Acknowledging the other faculty buildings on the campus, which are mostly red, the sculpture department has been clad in a rust-red stone, blending with its neighbours while creating a distinct identity. The accented use of cement recalls the building traditions of the wider Chongqing area and the common use of sand plaster. The façade also sports weathered aluminium board, which was made by students in the print department.

Overall, the volume expresses a dignified and rough aesthetic that conveys a sculptural spirit and the nature of the sculptural process.

Above and below
The site plan and elevation treatment highlight the architectural challenges presented by the confined footprint.

Opposite
The building façade is shaped to increase the daylight reaching the classroom spaces.

SONGYUE KINDERGARTEN, XIAMEN, FUJIAN

LUO SIWEI, 1998–2001

This project was driven by a recognition of the importance of understanding children. The architect believes in designing spaces that are specific to their patterns of thinking and behaviour.

Studies and observations have demonstrated that kindergarten design could be improved if the process were more focused on the environment rather than the space. A similar train of thought applies to structure rather than form, self-organized activities and not those organized by adults, uncertainty rather than certainty, imperfection as opposed to perfection, process instead of result, and experience rather than explanation.

The architecture of Songyue Kindergarten aspires to these fundamental principles. Square in plan, owing to the constraints of its surroundings, and with a total floor area of 2390 square metres, the structure is separated into functional zones by three courtyards, interspersing classrooms and offices with play areas. At ground level, the courtyard and open landscape spill out of the school building, providing sufficient space to accommodate a whole range of children's activities, both organized and spontaneous. Meticulous attention is applied to the landscaping detail. Soft and hard finishes provide flexibility for different uses,

and chequerboard designs inspire the invention of games.

The fused relationship between the interiors and the series of courtyards stems from the architect's understanding of Suzhou gardens. Borrowed views, controlled vistas and layers of contrast between scale, colour and form provide stimulation and excitement for learning, prompting the children to explore and discover their world.

Fun-injected learning is encouraged so that play is not limited to movement but is also influenced by touching, listening, smelling and observing. With the right complexity of architecture and the

appropriate assimilation of spatial relationships, playing becomes completely intuitive, informing the senses. The environment provides a framework in which the children can devise their own play methods.

Below
Vistas through controlled openings and wall cutouts allow glimpses of spaces beyond.

Opposite
Strategic colour elements and the fusion of indoor and outdoor spaces create a stimulating environment for exploring and learning.

TEACHING BUILDING, GRADUATE DEPARTMENT, CHINESE ACADEMY OF SCIENCE, ZHONG GUANCUN, BEIJING

INSTITUTE OF ARCHITECTURE DESIGN & RESEARCH, CHINESE ACADEMY OF SCIENCE, 2001–03

This award-winning project inherits many of its values from the other buildings on the campus, yet it is far from typical of education buildings. The architects primarily sought to create continuity and unity in style and form. The building's spirit comes from a desire to express the hi-tech character of the Zhong Guancun district, and a need for rationality, elegance and logic in terms of functional layout and material quality.

Red brick, a material that is often used in traditional education-campus buildings, is employed for emphasis on the façade of the Teaching Building. However, a subtle grid of windows creates an unusual architectural language while meeting the need for modulated natural light inside and acting as an effective barrier against external noise. Glass is the supporting dominant material, creating a crisply modern edge to the building form in expressing connecting elements such as the stairwell components and central atrium corridor.

Design is intended to reflect the information age, the expansion of knowledge and the growth of digital technology, emphasizing the spirit of communication and innovation. The backbone to the building is formed by a glass-ceilinged circulation spine along which the various departmental functions are distributed. The tilted walls adjoining the main entrance provide an air of openness, filtering natural light into the lobby and forming a gesture towards the rest of the campus buildings.

Right
A rendering reveals the strong linearity of the teaching building.

The central glass spine creates naturally lit internal spaces intersected by floating walkways.

Opposite
Extruded features emphasize the inner logic of the plan. The tilted wall panels adjoining the canopied front entrance suggest openness.

TIANJIN TAIDA PRIMARY SCHOOL, TIANJIN

CHINA ARCHITECTURE DESIGN & RESEARCH GROUP, 1999–2001

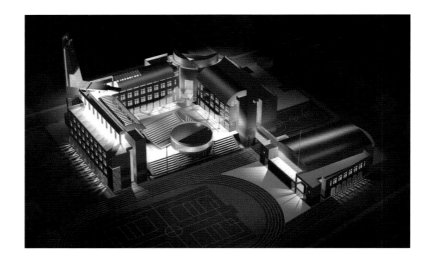

The Tianjin Taida Primary School sets a new benchmark for educational architecture in China. China Architecture Design & Research Group was asked to investigate the inner nature of the school and the identity that it seeks to project to the community. The design revolves around the composition of key geometric elements, beginning with a circular moon-gate entrance, a highly symbolic gesture often found in traditional Chinese architecture. Here, a modern interpretation of the motif sets the tone for what lies beyond.

Architecturally, the design explores the relationship between solid and void. Rather than designating the heart of the school as a single, solid entity, the centrepiece is an open space. The teaching and office blocks embrace this square courtyard on three sides, creating a protective environment for the children. At the nucleus of the courtyard is a sunken open arena that can be used as an amphitheatre for student celebrations, performances and festivals. However, it also serves as a less formal outdoor teaching facility and as a forum for exchange between students and teachers.

Particular attention was paid to the penetration of natural light in the building, and some of the teaching spaces spill out on to the inner courtyard platform. Beneath the circular music hall, an activity room is fitted with a series of sliding glass doors that can be folded back into the playground. This is particularly useful for hosting grand ceremonies and large functions.

The student spaces are treated with a stimulating palette of materials, selected for durability and low maintenance. Colour accents signal particular functions, while other areas are left without texture or tone. These provide a blank backdrop for children to explore art through sculpture and colourful wall canvases.

Opposite
An aerial perspective of the school development highlights the complex relationships between functions.

The inner spaces allow an interplay of natural light, colour and texture.

Above
The school buildings are orientated around a central courtyard.

Right
The moon gate creates a formal sense of entrance.

WENZHENG COLLEGE LIBRARY, SUZHOU UNIVERSITY, YUE XI, WU XIAN, SUZHOU

AMATEUR ARCHITECTURE STUDIO, 1998–2000

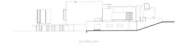

site plan & second floor plan

Occupying some 4000 square metres of countryside, Wenzheng College Library, part of Suzhou University, originated in a competition. The winning scheme, by Wang Shu, Lu Wenyu and Tong Ming, was designed with the purpose of connecting its users to the surrounding mountains and water, recalling the style of Suzhou gardens.

The three-storey library has a floor area of 9000 square metres. With mountains to the rear, facing north, scattered with lush bamboo, the hilly site slopes south down to the water with a 4-metre difference in levels. The body of water started life as an abandoned brick field. Faced with this unique site, the architects, working in association with the Suzhou Construction Group, followed the traditional principles of garden design by minimizing the prominence of the buildings between mountains and water. This explains why almost half of the reinforced-concrete framework is sunk below ground level. The lower level of the building is submerged. The south-facing main linear building is elevated over the water, and orientated to maximize the benefits of the prevailing summer breezes. Four other buildings, smaller in scale, accommodate additional facilities and are terraced down the site from north to south.

A simple palette of materials is applied to the flat-roofed framed boxes. Ramps and pathways link the buildings as they step down to the water. Referring again to Chinese gardens, the emphasis is on altering the scale of elements as one moves through the landscape. The appearance of the pavilion-style buildings, perched over the water, reinforces the underlying principle of the architecture, that of man and nature in perfect balance.

Opposite
Elevations and plans emphasize the architecture's empathy with its context.

Meandering circulation paths encourage users to explore the site fully.

Above and right
The library buildings perch over the water in a close relationship with nature.

YANCHENG MEDICAL SCHOOL LIBRARY, YANCHENG, JIANGSU

ZHU JINGXIANG STUDIO, 2001–03

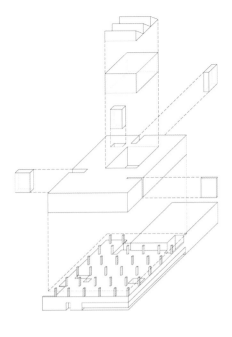

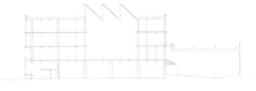

The new 7000-square-metre library of Yancheng Medical School is sited next to the Main Lecture Building. The Lecture Building was completed in 1998 and is connected to the new structure by a skywalk that projects from the library at first-floor level. The scheme goes some way towards realizing the school's plan for a covered internal circulation system on campus, which started with the design of the main lecture building in 1996. The suspended walkway is treated by the architects as a raised artificial ground plane, and its form is inspired by reflecting features of the surrounding landscape.

In fact, the library can easily be accessed at true ground level from the campus plaza to the west, which is separated from the nearby street to the east. However, once they are transported to the sky-bridge, users get unobstructed views in both directions. Above this artificial ground, functional reading spaces radiate around a three-storey atrium covered by a sawtooth roof. The openings in the roof and the various heights and forms that are juxtaposed to the vertical void contribute to the natural illumination and ventilation of the interior.

A 350-seat auditorium can be reached from the ground and first floors. Its balcony takes advantage of a cantilevered overhang on the main body of the building, which canopies over the entrance. This and other compositional features of the library can be easily understood through the distinctive use of materials. The floating mass is clad with granite. Dark tile is applied to the cuboid auditorium and podium surface facing the street. Aluminium panels clad the cantilevered slab, and white paint outlines the distinctive columns.

Glass is used in several ways, fulfilling several functions. To prevent direct sunlight from entering the reading areas and to reduce the effects of solar gain, most openings are filled with translucent double-glazing. Transparent glass is strategically placed, based on calculations of view and light intensity. The double-height glazing of the entrance enforces the overall image of the library, while allowing the spatial organization of the building to be perceived vertically.

Right and opposite
The substantial new library has been fitted seamlessly into the campus, accessed at first-floor level by a covered walkway that fulfils the school's plan for an enclosed circulation system.

YANCHENG YOUTH CENTRE, YANCHENG, JIANGSU

ZHU JINGXIANG STUDIO, 1997–2000

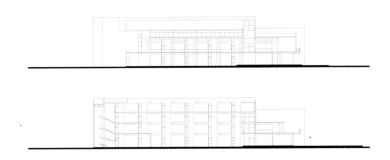

Located in a peripheral part of Yancheng in Jiangsu Province, the site of the Yancheng Youth Centre is fringed by reed marshes, irrigation ditches and modest farm housing. The building's flexible layout makes it suitable for use as a school, research centre or small gallery. The functions accommodated range from studios to a dormitory, canteen, kitchen, office, indoor sports hall and roof garden. It has been designed to allow as much daylight and natural ventilation as possible inside.

The project evolved from the idea of a multifunctional building to meet the tenants'

different needs. In plan, it is segregated into north and south segments, one relating to more public and high-energy uses, and the other dedicated to individual activities that require silent, unitary spaces. Where the two components overlap, between the edges of the atrium and the ventilation ducts, a buffer zone is defined. It is delineated by a series of deep and shallow cavities interspersed with voids or chinks of light and a different floor treatment.

Corridors and stairs wrap the two ends of the space. Navigating the stairs challenges users with a variety of surprising

visual experiences, veering between openness and enclosure. Differences in floor heights add to the complexity of the perception of the space.

Considering that the building functions as a youth centre, the temptation would be to use fashionable materials and finishes. However, the architect refused to follow this path. Even local materials, such as terrazzo, are used in an unexpected form and colour.

Designing the building to achieve a comfortable environment in the adverse local climate was a principal consideration. The architect adopted a low-tech approach,

in keeping with the building's rural context and the limited budget. Effective measures include the cantilevered brise-soleil, ventilation chimneys and an additional wall to buffer the winter winds.

Above and below
Sections and interior views emphasize the layering of vistas throughout the building.

Opposite
External features, such as the cantilevered brise-soleil and wind-protection wall, shield the building against the adverse climate.

BANK OF CHINA HEAD OFFICE BUILDING, BEIJING
PEI PARTNERSHIP ARCHITECTS

BEIJING BOOKS BUILDING, CHANG'AN AVENUE, BEIJING
OMA

BRIGHT DAIRY HEADQUARTERS, WU ZHONG ROAD, SHANGHAI
ARQUITECTONICA

THE BUND CENTER, SHANGHAI
JOHN PORTMAN & ASSOCIATES

CCTV HEADQUARTERS, BEIJING
OMA

CHEMSUNNY PLAZA, CHANG'AN AVENUE, BEIJING
SKIDMORE, OWINGS & MERRILL

CHINA ELECTRONICS CORPORATION PLAZA, BEIJING
NBBJ

**CHINA NATURAL OFFSHORE OIL CORPORATION
HEADQUARTERS, DONGCHENG, BEIJING**
KOHN PEDERSEN FOX ASSOCIATES

CLOUD NINE MALL, CHANGNING ROAD, SHANGHAI
ARQUITECTONICA

DIGITAL BEIJING, BEIJING
URBANUS ARCHITECTURE AND DESIGN

**GATE TO THE EAST – TWIN TOWERS DEVELOPMENT,
SUZHOU INDUSTRIAL TECHNOLOGY PARK, SUZHOU**
RMJM HK

**HANGZHOU LAKESHORE DEVELOPMENT,
HANGZHOU, ZHEJIANG**
THE JERDE PARTNERSHIP

**HEBEI EDUCATION PUBLISHING HOUSE,
SHIJIAZHUANG, HEBEI**
ATELIER FEICHANG JIANZHU

**JIE FANG DAILY NEWS HEADQUARTERS,
HENAN ROAD, SHANGHAI**
KAPLAN MCLAUGHLIN DIAZ

JIUSHI HEADQUARTERS, PUDONG, SHANGHAI
FOSTER AND PARTNERS

LAN HUA INTERNATIONAL BUILDING, BEIJING
LEIGH & ORANGE

NINGBO Y-TOWN, NINGBO
MADA S.P.A.M.

PLAZA 66, NANJING XI LU, SHANGHAI
KOHN PEDERSEN FOX ASSOCIATES

R&F CENTRE, GUANGZHOU
AEDAS

SHANGHAI WORLD FINANCIAL CENTER, PUDONG, SHANGHAI
KOHN PEDERSEN FOX ASSOCIATES

SHENZHEN URBAN-PLANNING BUREAU OFFICE, SHENZHEN
URBANUS ARCHITECTURE AND DESIGN

SHOPPING YARD, LANGFANG CITY, HEBEI
JINAO KANN FINCH DESIGN GROUP

SOHO SHANG DU, DONGDAQIAO LU, BEIJING
LAB ARCHITECTURE STUDIO

SONGSANGHU CITY HOUSE, DONGGUAN, GUANGDONG
QIXIN ARCHITECTS AND ENGINEERS

THREE ON THE BUND, SHANGHAI
MICHAEL GRAVES & ASSOCIATES

**TIANJIN HUASHI OFFICE BUILDING, TIANJIN DAGANG
POWER PLANT, TIANJIN**
XWG (BEIJING TSINGHUA ARCHITECTURAL DESIGN & CONSULTATION)

TOMORROW SQUARE, SHANGHAI
JOHN PORTMAN & ASSOCIATES

**WANGJING SCIENCE & TECHNOLOGY CAMPUS – SECOND PHASE,
WANGJING, BEIJING**
BEIJING INSTITUTE OF ARCHITECTURAL DESIGN

XINTIANDI, SHANGHAI
WOOD AND ZAPATA

YIN TAI CENTRE, BEIJING
JOHN PORTMAN & ASSOCIATES

ZHONG GUANCUN WEST, HAI DIAN, BEIJING
KOHN PEDERSEN FOX ASSOCIATES

BANK OF CHINA HEAD OFFICE BUILDING, BEIJING

PEI PARTNERSHIP ARCHITECTS, 1995–2001

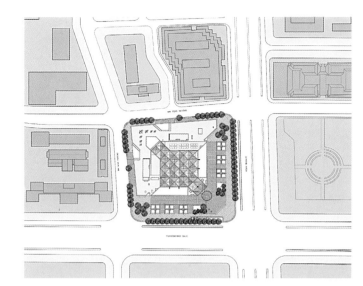

Described as a building that balances time, place and purpose with spatial complexity, structural stability and quality execution, the Bank of China's head office is intended to enrich the city and its community through a harmonious balance between architecture and nature. Its innovative design looks into the future while building on the cultural roots of the past.

The building is both open and inviting. The site's diagonal orientation to the revered Temple of Heaven and the physical and metaphorical attributes of its location as a gateway to Beijing's new financial district have shaped many aspects of the project's design and layout.

The 175,000-square-metre structure manages to accommodate more than three thousand employees, a two-thousand-seat auditorium, a monumental banking hall, reception hall, dining and other service functions, and stay within central Beijing's 45.7-metre height limit. Recalling the planning of traditional Chinese courtyard houses, the offices frame an interior atrium that is landscaped with water, rocks and plants in simplified form and modest scale. As the building's functional and symbolic core, the atrium illuminates and animates the spaces around it while maximizing open space and natural light,

and creating a lantern effect at night.

Clad in honey-coloured travertine, the exterior conveys solidity and stability, reinforcing the fabric of the streetscape in a city that is historically defined by its walls. Large recesses at the base of the eleven-storey executive wing demarcate the front entrances, which are spanned by double-height 49-metre-long trusses weighing 200 tons. This wing houses the bank's nerve centres: its 24-hour foreign-exchange trading room and a high-tech global network-control facility.

Planned as two L-shaped wings embracing the 3000-square-metre garden court, the executive offices front the building's major thoroughfares. A glass wall rises 59 metres at the junction of the executive wing, welcoming patrons and gesturing towards the temple. It restricts entry yet maintains expansive views of the banking halls opposite the other wing. The two banking halls are connected by a circular lightwell and linked directly to the atrium, forming a gateless space that is both open and secure. The upper-level banking hall is vertically orientated towards the dramatic skylight overhead, its glassy, diaphanous structure contrasting with the gridded surrounding walls.

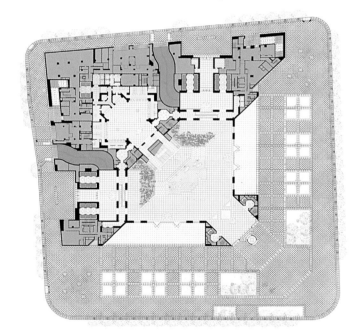

Right
The site plan, floor plan and a section reveal the succession of functional spaces in relation to the internal atrium.

Opposite
The exterior of the Head Office Building is designed to convey solidity.

The internal garden oasis is formed by a glass-enclosed atrium.

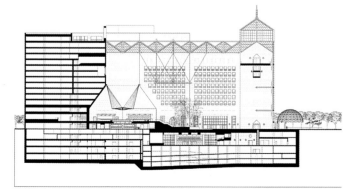

BEIJING BOOKS BUILDING, CHANG'AN AVENUE, BEIJING

OMA, 2003–07

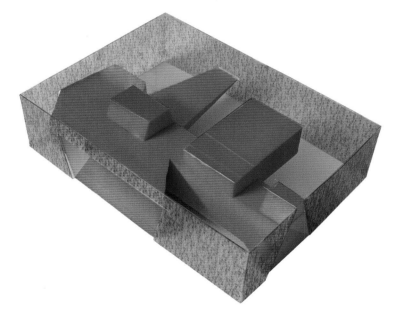

The commission for this new bookshop followed an invited competition in 2003, orchestrated by the client, Beijing Xinha Books. Dutch architect Rem Koolhaas of OMA knows much about the art of shopping, having completed flagship shops for the international luxury fashion market. While a bookshop may present a different angle on the activities of shoppers, Koolhaas makes the same connections.

Shopping patterns are changing with increasing velocity, to the extent that OMA believes that shopping has become an introverted activity. Research leads the practice to believe that retail environments should frequently be housed in closed boxes where, counterintuitively, less of their contents are revealed. Furthermore, the larger the store, the less its volume appears to communicate the essence of the events taking place inside.

At the Beijing Books Building, the 100,000-square-metre site is divided between a new 48,000-square-metre structure and the converted existing retail space, comprising 52,000 square metres. In its existing state, the bookshop has heavy traffic and is intensively used. The heightened activity creates a wave of energy, but little of it is projected to the cityscape beyond.

In the process of doubling the scale of the building, and with the addition of new public and technological elements, the intensity of the store is likely to increase to explosive levels. The architects' intention is to search for a way to channel this energy within the building, exploiting these forces by revolutionizing the way the store's shopping is organized, and devising a method to convey this dynamic to the city.

OMA has 'mastered' the enlarged volume by carving out a cruciform void that opens out to Chang'an Avenue while also offering a huge, symbolic 'window' to Xi Dan Cultural Plaza. Internally, the intersecting void allows clear circulation paths to be defined. The architects describe it as two interior boulevards, which also contain the most public functions of the programme. The distribution of activities is configured from the middle floor, reducing the distance between the various book departments. The 'window' is both a façade and an electronic billboard, broadcasting events inside the building to the outside, while news and information from the rest of the world is transmitted inside.

Opposite
Various exterior views emphasize the carved elevations of the building.

The oversized 'window' façade is also an electronic billboard.

Above
A section and partial axonometric reveal the intersecting void and the internal boulevard.

BRIGHT DAIRY HEADQUARTERS, WU ZHONG ROAD, SHANGHAI

ARQUITECTONICA, 2000–01

The brief from China's largest dairy products group, Bright Dairy, required Florida-based practice Arquitectonica to design a new headquarters office complex that would reflect its standing in the industry and project a clear corporate image. The commission was complicated by the need to accommodate a partially constructed building already on the site. The architects managed to overcome this constraint and have created an arrangement of structures that meets the company's aspirations, providing an open and welcoming environment that evokes the company's ethos.

Essentially, the headquarters design segregates the functional components of the programme into two distinct main zones: a lower courtyard block containing the more open and public functions, and a taller structure to the rear that houses the main administrative offices.

Forming the focal element of the complex, a large gold truncated cone announces the building to the street and signals the gateway to the main entrance.

This structure is also distinguished functionally, housing the company's main boardroom. Its form creates a counterpoint to the cylindrical void beyond that occupies the heart of the complex. This courtyard is open to the sky and surrounded by a gently rising spiral walkway that eventually culminates in a large multifunctional area that can be used to host special events. The ascending journey presents an opportunity to create a gallery space along the route, showcasing images and exhibits from the company's history.

The centre of the courtyard is dominated by an over-scaled glass torch, abstracted from the company's logo. This provides a sculptural centrepiece to the inner core of the building. Though the private office spaces are accessed from their own separate circulation system, the taller rear block also shares views down into the central courtyard. The façade of this block is articulated by irregularly angled glazing mullions, and forms a lively backdrop to the forms that wrap the lower courtyard block.

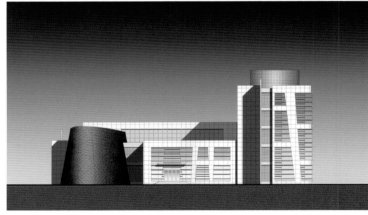

Right
An aerial perspective and rendering of the east elevation show how the architects have managed to accommodate a number of structures on the site.

Opposite
The approach to the main entrance shows the truncated conical structure that forms the focal point of the complex.

Natural light penetrates the inner courtyard and boardroom.

THE BUND CENTER, SHANGHAI

JOHN PORTMAN & ASSOCIATES, 1995–2002

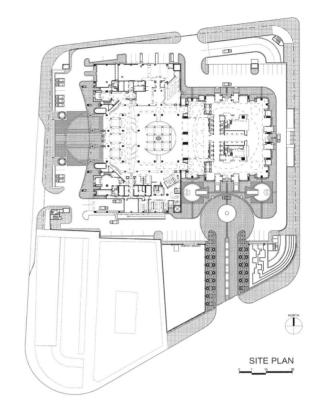

SITE PLAN

Lodged neatly behind the historic financial quarter of the Bund with its heritage architecture, the Bund Center is a sizable mixed-use high-rise complex containing a forty-five-storey office tower, the 303-guestroom Westin Hotel and a serviced apartment building.

The hotel incorporates extensive business services, including conference suites and meeting rooms totalling 1586 square metres, and regularly hosts international events. It also features dining, entertainment, spa and recreation amenities.

The development's modern character is subtly infused with Chinese cultural elements. Particular emphasis is given to the top of the building with the lotus-inspired crown. This 582.5-ton feature is composed of a ring, symbolizing eternity, supporting two concentric layers of petals that stretch up more than 11 metres and signify growth and prosperity. At night, lighting draws attention to this powerful emblem and the distinctive profile of the tower against the city skyline.

The Bund Center is conceived as Puxi's major financial hub and therefore heralds a greater sense of civic pride than its functional programme implies. As building in the historic context demands enormous sensitivity, a collection of relatively small eclectic structures was considered more appropriate than a single dominating tower. This approach also gave the architect more scope to incorporate the various ideas that a project of this prominence and importance brings to the drawing board.

The central tower is flanked on either side by the shorter twenty-six-storey Westin Hotel and Westin Residences. Clean symmetrical forms and formal articulation of materials and vocabulary respond to the urban fabric. The composition embraces the streetscape and invites public appreciation.

Right
The site plan reveals the collection of eclectic structures that comprise the Bund Center.

The view from across the Huangpu River shows the landmark tower behind the historic Bund district.

A detail shows the streamlined form of the façade.

Opposite
The lotus-inspired crown lends the tower a distinctive profile.

CCTV HEADQUARTERS, BEIJING

OMA, 2002–08

The new headquarters building for the Central Chinese Television network will be among the first of about three hundred towers that are expected to erupt in Beijing's emerging Central Business District. The winning scheme, by Dutch architectural practice OMA, was picked from submissions by ten practices following an invited international competition organized by the Beijing International Tendering Company. A jury that included architect Arata Isozaki and critic Charles Jencks selected three teams for the second phase: Toyo Ito & Associates in collaboration with FCJZ of Beijing, the East China Architectural Design & Research Institute, and OMA.

Planned for completion before the Beijing Olympic Games, the winning proposal is being realized in collaboration with the East China Architectural Design & Research Institute from Shanghai. OMA has involved its media and research branch, AMO, as well as structural and mechanical engineering expertise from Arup.

The scheme consolidates the project's programme in an iconic configuration of two high-rise structures on a 10-hectare site. With a height of 230 metres and enclosing a floor area of 405,000 square metres, the CCTV building will house facilities that encompass the complete process of TV-programme making. Administration, news, broadcasting, studios and programme-production functions are organized as a series of interconnected activities.

The unorthodox composition of the tower – with its continuous looping structure – establishes a different relationship with the street than that of a traditional commercial skyscraper, creating an urban setting rather than a single, skyward profile. The irregular grid on the building's façades is an expression of the forces travelling throughout its structure.

A second building accommodates the 116,000-square-metre Television Cultural Centre (TVCC) and includes a hotel, a visitor centre, a large public theatre and exhibition spaces. It is visible from the main intersection of the Central Business District through the framed 'window' opening of the CCTV Headquarters. A media park forms a landscape of public entertainment, outdoor filming areas and production studios as an extension of the central green axis of the city's key business hub.

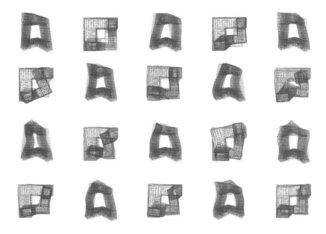

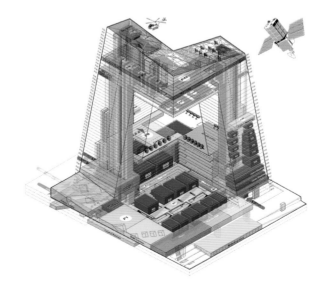

CHEMSUNNY PLAZA, CHANG'AN AVENUE, BEIJING

SKIDMORE, OWINGS & MERRILL, 2004–06

Located on a high-profile site in the heart of the city, the project's architecture had to meet the demands for continuity with existing buildings, setbacks, height limitations and public spaces, as well as complying with zoning requirements that determine the overall building massing. Tradition and technology, both highly revered in China, provided a platform for SOM to explore new architectural forms within the context of Chinese symbolism. The building's identity is expressed through its composition and the use of new materials, technology and building systems.

The office accommodation comprises three parallel bars connected by two atriums and four bridges. This approach allows the solid components to be used as tenanted offices, while the void of the atrium forms a semi-public realm, drawing the public plaza on Chang'an Avenue into the building's core. The solid and void elements become interlocked and increasingly complex through the introduction of a second layer that penetrates the basic form and void. Like the interconnected pieces of a Chinese puzzle, as elements are removed, space is revealed and a new mass emerges. With further elements stripped away, abstract relationships between one space and another are formed.

In Chinese pictographs, separate components are combined to form one complete character with its own inclusive meaning and sound. By working in reverse to break down the building's composition, the architects reveal the interdependence of horizontal and vertical lines. To instil discipline in the compositions of voids and solids, the vocabulary is limited to I, L and Z forms, patterns that are derived from traditional Chinese art and calligraphy in their most primitive state.

The architectural language is legible in the external articulation, the floorplate configuration, the section and the atrium elevation. Offices link through the atrium to create large contiguous floorplates on the bridge floors, allowing multistorey windows that maximize natural light in the atrium. Pools at ground level recycle water while reflecting light back into the interior; their placement heightens the sense of movement from one zone to another.

For internal comfort, the façade comprises two layers of glass separated by an interstitial ventilated space that removes trapped warm air. Solar-control elements prevent the sun's heat from entering occupied zones, and the openable glazing enables users to obtain tempered fresh air from outside.

Opposite
Various elevation perspectives illustrate the complex solid and void formations that permeate the architecture.

Left
The internal atrium – a semi-public realm connected with the street – is enlivened with protruding volumes and interlocking bridges.

中国电子

CHINA ELECTRONICS CORPORATION PLAZA, BEIJING

NBBJ, 2003–05

Designed for the largest electronics conglomerate in China, this commercial office tower is the company's headquarters building. Located in a new technology park outside Beijing, the site is governed by a masterplan laid down in the West Zone of Zhong Guancun, and outlined in a regulatory document titled 'Controlling Construction Conditions for the Planning Blocks'. NBBJ's goal was to distil the cultural energy and dynamism of China Electronics Corporation within the limits of the project's programme and the constraints of the masterplan.

The architecture is defined by three interlocking elements that together comprise 84,000 square metres. Diversity and energy is invested in each form. The gently curving East Building provides a stable background to and strong direction towards the heart of the technology park and is the cornerstone of the complex. The West Building incorporates the company's products division, and the third element is an open space designed for the company's employees, organized round an atrium that connects the two technology buildings and functions as a gathering place for the exchange of ideas.

Two of the buildings stand on a north–south axis at the edge of the east and west property lines. The West Building is twenty-one storeys high and the East Building is seventeen. Their orientation balances the site's composition and allows green open space to be integrated on the south-west and north-east areas, retaining the radial pattern of the masterplan.

From the south, entry to the development is via a four-storey atrium that forms the base of the building composition. It provides orientation to the buildings from the connecting terraces from the north and east, as required by the masterplan. The complementary forms of the East and West Buildings are integrated at the base by the four-storey atrium, and complete a composition that collectively generates movement and energy.

The atrium anchors the complex and with its sweeping roof and glass wall pulls the architecture round the south-west corner into the technology park. It weaves under the East Building to the north and becomes the major entry for the level-two terrace connections from the north and east. Glass, shaded glass and metal façades include sunshading on the western exposure to reduce solar gain.

Opposite and left
The substantial office complex comprises three linked buildings, including a heavily glazed atrium that gives access on to a landscaped plaza.

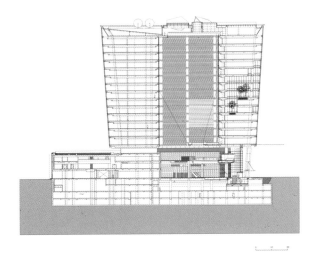

GROUND FLOOR PLAN

CHINA NATURAL OFFSHORE OIL CORPORATION HEADQUARTERS, DONGCHENG, BEIJING

KOHN PEDERSEN FOX ASSOCIATES, 2002–05

This eighteen-storey headquarters building is located at a major crossroads along the Second Ring Road in Beijing's eastern Dongcheng district. It comprises 65,000 square metres above ground and 29,000 square metres below. The triangular site is on a corner opposite the massive Ministry of Foreign Affairs Building, to which Kohn Pedersen Fox's design creates a distinctly urban counterpoint.

Images of offshore oil production are conveyed by the building's three-sided, curvaceous and glassy form. The prow-like shape suggests an oil-tanker's bow without resorting to literal motifs or materials. Its mass is elevated off the ground and shifted at an angle to the base component, a reminder of an offshore oil derrick. The effect is further magnified by the design of the ground plane, which has been developed to suggest the ocean's surface.

A full-height skylit central atrium organizes the peripheral office and function spaces. The skylight and clerestory windows at the top allow filtered light to penetrate inside. In addition, portions of the upper floorplates have been removed to create large sky-gardens that draw daylight into the atrium from all three sides. These breathing spaces are individually designed and positioned in response to the path of the sun on each elevation.

The triangular tower is rounded at the edges and uses a glass curtain-wall system. Its rotation in relation to the podium it sits on maximizes the benefits of the site, creating the opportunity for an entrance courtyard along the quieter edge of the building. This is entered through a symbolic gateway that recalls traditional Chinese structures. The three-storey L-shaped podium, finished in custom-made terracotta tiles, helps to define this plaza and integrates the development's more public realms, such as meeting rooms, restaurants and exhibition areas.

Opposite
The site plan and a section through the building reveal that its three sides are wrapped around a full-height atrium.

The aerodynamic form of the triangular tower presents a foil to the surrounding buildings.

Left
The atrium organizes the surrounding office functions and creates landscaped open space.

CLOUD NINE MALL, CHANGNING ROAD, SHANGHAI

ARQUITECTONICA, 2001–06

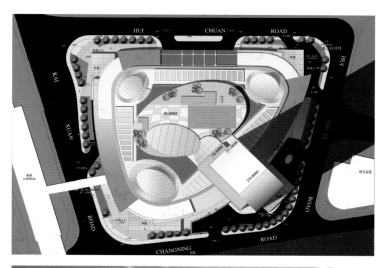

As Shanghai continues its rapid growth, an integrated transport strategy is an essential component of its sustainable development plan. Cloud Nine Mall is a multiple-use development that integrates a nine-level retail mall with 22,000 square metres of office space and a 700-room five-star hotel. Most significantly, it also serves as a major public-transport interchange.

Designed by Florida-based practice Arquitectonica, the project sits at the intersection of one of Shanghai's subway lines and the elevated light railway, providing a direct link between the two. The large podium also encompasses a triple-line bus terminus and a major taxi rank, with additional parking areas below ground for 850 cars and 2000 bicycles. The curved exterior of the podium expresses the internal organization of the mall and evokes the dynamics of travel, wrapping the retail space in a spiralling movement of copper-tinged overlapping forms.

Rising up from one side of the podium is the combined office and hotel tower. The two functions are clearly expressed in its form: a lower angled volume, clad entirely in black glass, intersects with the graceful curve of a taller blue volume. The intersection of forms provides the choice of larger floorplates for office tenants while anchoring the soaring 240-metre-high main hotel volume to the podium. The volumes are further differentiated through random streaks of light within the curtain wall – horizontally in the taller, blue volume, and vertically in the lower, black volume.

The retail portion of the complex includes three food courts, a multiscreen cinema, department stores, supermarket and speciality shops, covering a total of 150,000 square metres. Orientation and circulation within such a large mall is a major challenge. It is resolved by column-free linear atrium walkways that connect three elliptical corner atrium spaces and together form a simple closed loop around a central core of vertically stacked department stores. Escalators are located in the main corner atriums and criss-cross upwards through these monumental voids, allowing customers clear views and easy wayfinding. Vast skylights let natural light permeate down through every level of the mall.

Opposite
An aerial perspective shows the complex illuminated at night.

Flooded with natural light from the expansive skylight, the column-free spaces promote visibility and easy orientation.

Left
The site plan details the functional components of the complex.

An exterior view highlights the distinctive articulation of the hotel/office tower.

DIGITAL BEIJING, BEIJING
URBANUS ARCHITECTURE AND DESIGN, 2003–06

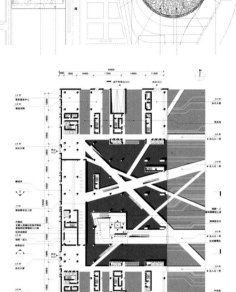

With the Beijing Olympics set for 2008, the municipal government is committed to presenting the most technologically sophisticated content ever witnessed in the history of the games. The Digital Beijing building will serve as the formal headquarters and data centre for the games. The programme marries this with office, exhibition and museum spaces totalling 96,000 square metres.

Located at the northern end of the central axis of the Olympic site, the rectilinear site occupies a prominent position close to the Olympics Centre, National Stadium and National Swimming Center. The task of designing Digital Beijing was awarded following an invited international competition involving seven well-known practices. The winning proposal was presented by a team comprising Urbanus Architecture and Design and the China Institute of Building Standards Design and Research. Their design was conceived as a landmark that would represent the fast-moving and ever-evolving digital era. Before the building operates in

its official capacity during the games, it will be used as a virtual museum and exhibition centre for manufacturers of digital equipment.

The design team focused on the meaning of contemporary architecture in the context of digital information and digitally enhanced experiences. The surface of the building is envisaged as a changing canvas, conveying the dynamic scenography of the digital Olympics as they happen. The building is treated as an object that is continually redefining itself, perpetually being renewed as it keeps pace with the times. Its articulation is an abstraction of technologically inspired imagery – digital barcodes, integrated-circuit boards, the simple alternating repetition of zero and one. These are juxtaposed with the more familiar and poetic reality of water. The potent combination is emphasized through the depiction of a magnified digital world, referring to elements such as the microchip that are so prevalent in our daily lives yet so invisible.

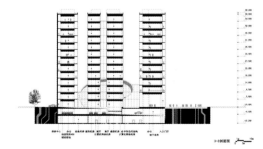

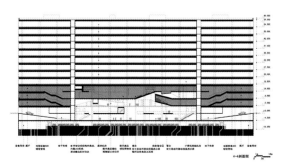

Right
Plans and sections illustrate the complex layering of the architecture.

Opposite
The envelope design stems from digitally inspired imagery.

Interior spaces combine office, exhibition and museum facilities.

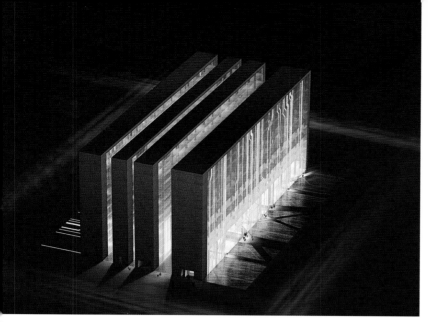

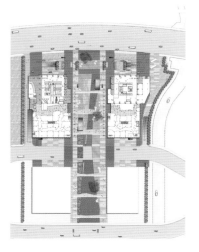

GATE TO THE EAST – TWIN TOWERS DEVELOPMENT, SUZHOU INDUSTRIAL TECHNOLOGY PARK, SUZHOU

RMJM HK, 2004–08

Opposite
An aerial perspective depicts the joined Twin Towers development in relation to the waterfront and the surrounding landscape.

Above
At ground level, the complex is planned around civic gardens and plazas.

Below
The overlay roof design provides a seamless frame to the top of the arch.

The 278-metre-tall gateway building designed by RMJM will be China's largest single building in terms of gross floor area. Spearheaded by the Tian Di Group, a private local developer, the building is conceived as a landmark entrance to the New Suzhou Central Business District (CBD), part of the Suzhou Industrial Technology Park. This is an ambitious joint venture between the Chinese and Singaporean governments to create a 7000-hectare modern industrial park similar to Singapore's Jurong Town.

The architect's intention was for the structure to convey a simple reverence and respect for China's culture and history. The Suzhou Twin Towers provide a dramatic icon that not only signals the entrance

to the new city, but is also a symbolic 'gateway to the east', representing the significance of the new China in today's world. As the focal point of the new Central Business District, the Twin Towers have drawn inspiration from the famed traditional gardens of Suzhou in the form of the 'moon gate' or 'vase door' that announces thresholds or transitions.

The building is designed to complement the urban fabric: landscaped pedestrian zones are woven through the tower, culminating in the presidential garden suites at the top. Pedestrian promenades also join the new development seamlessly with the shores of Jinji Lake.

The joined towers, with their grand arch extending to the CBD axis towards

the lake, have a streamlined geometry. The higher floors have a wider frontage towards the lake, maximizing floor areas with lake views. Two sheaths of curtain wall gently overlay the tower, smoothing the contours of the form like a veil of Suzhou silk.

The mixed-use complex will house a 450-room five-star hotel and a platinum five-star hotel, office accommodation, a serviced apartment block and a 100,000-square-metre shopping mall. Because of the project's semi-public role as a civic structure, it delivers a new kind of commercially viable public environment, enriched with inviting places. It will be central to the development of the New Suzhou CBD and Jinji Lake District.

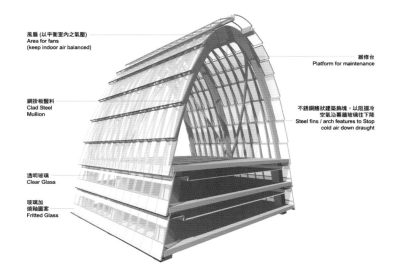

風扇 (以平衡室內之氣壓)
Area for fans
(keep indoor air balanced)

維修台
Platform for maintenance

鋼掛板醫料
Clad Steel
Mullion

不銹鋼鰭狀建築飾塊，以阻擋冷
空氣沿幕牆玻璃往下降
Steel fins / arch features to Stop
cold air down draught

透明玻璃
Clear Glass

玻璃加
燒軸圖案
Fritted Glass

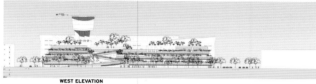

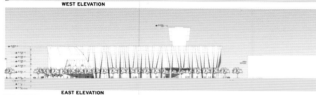

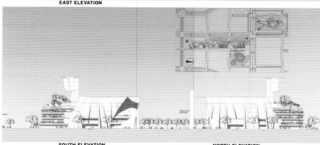

WEST ELEVATION

EAST ELEVATION

SOUTH ELEVATION NORTH ELEVATION

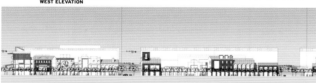

WEST ELEVATION

EAST ELEVATION

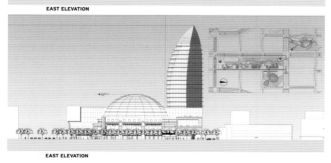

EAST ELEVATION

HANGZHOU LAKESHORE DEVELOPMENT, HANGZHOU, ZHEJIANG

THE JERDE PARTNERSHIP, 2002–06

The original masterplan for Hangzhou Lakeshore Development mixes office, leisure, entertainment and retail uses. In co-ordination with Hangzhou's regeneration efforts, The Jerde Partnership has remodelled a blighted district of five city blocks near the waterfront into a new hub of urban activity.

Conceptually inspired by the transformative power of water, modern architecture is interwoven with natural elements such as the striking 'canyon' that is carved out of one of the city's blocks. With its expressive water landscape, the experience of the development becomes an extension of the lake's presence throughout Hangzhou, animating the shoreline and nurturing the emergence of an image from which redevelopment can grow.

One block of the project is designed around a central canal that extends West Lake into the heart of the city. In the original masterplan a man-made canal runs through and connects all aspects of the redevelopment. Recalling the city's ancient waterways, the canal carves a dynamic architectural 'canyon'. On the lake side, rich landscaping is blended with cafés and restaurants, including a boutique restaurant tower rising 50 metres with views of the development, the lake and the mountains beyond. On the city side of the canal, glass and man-made materials form a distinctly urban palette accommodating retail uses, restaurants and a cinema, accessed by bridges on several levels. This circulation mingles the natural and the urban, symbolically connecting the lake and the city.

Diagonally behind the canyon, the development takes on a more urban feel in the form of a three-block pedestrian street that is animated by day and by night. One side of the street is lined with reconstructed historic shop houses, while the other side features modern glass structures. Varying in height from two to five storeys, the glass structures will house offices, retail outlets and restaurants. At intervals along the three blocks the street opens into courtyards with upper-level terraces and public areas. The street will be covered by a light glass and steel canopy, protecting visitors from bad weather.

Opposite
Aerial and street-level perspectives highlight the natural and urban, historic and modern elements that are blended into the complex. The man-made canal refers to the city's ancient waterways and creates a distinct identity.

Left
The site plan establishes a contemporary urban framework for redevelopment, informed by the city's natural and historic character.

Elevations flanking either bank of the 'canyon' recall the city to one side and water to the other.

HEBEI EDUCATION PUBLISHING HOUSE, SHIJIAZHUANG, HEBEI

ATELIER FEICHANG JIANZHU, 2000–03

First Floor Plan

The 16,800-square-metre reinforced-concrete-frame structure enjoys relatively open waterfront views in the commercial district of Shijiazhuang. Hebei Education Publishing House specified a modern office building with a capacity far greater than the accommodation it needs for its own business.

The publishing operation is confined to the top three levels of the twelve-storey building. This horizontal structure hovers over the other floors and is articulated in a markedly different manner. The client's wish to exploit as fully as possible the potential of the site footprint, taking advantage of a buoyant real-estate market, led to a consideration of a wide range of uses: rented office units, conference and exhibition facilities – including a small art museum – guest accommodation, a restaurant, sports hall, café and bookstore.

To accommodate this unorthodox mix of uses, Atelier Feichang Jianzhu explored various relationships and roles. The resulting programme is strangely urban, a metaphor of the city in miniature. Loosely fragmented into three distinctive components, the head office bridges over the top of the two building wings, forming a shelter to the voids below. Its multilayered elevation adapts itself to the sun's path with moveable screens that form a varying façade pattern.

The wider footprints of the ground and first floors are reserved for larger spaces such as the basketball court, kitchens, restaurant and multipurpose hall. Further up the two supporting buildings, suspended bridges lace the structures together with a series of green walkways. A double-height sky-garden is sandwiched between the top of the eastern block and the publishing offices above. The relative openness of the structure allows the general public to penetrate its mass and explore this vertical urban garden.

Right
The first floor accommodates larger, communal facilities.

The horizontal head-office structure sits above the two building blocks and is treated as a distinct form.

Opposite
Screening devices clad the top three floors of the complex, creating a varied façade.

The two building halves are connected at different levels via sky-bridges.

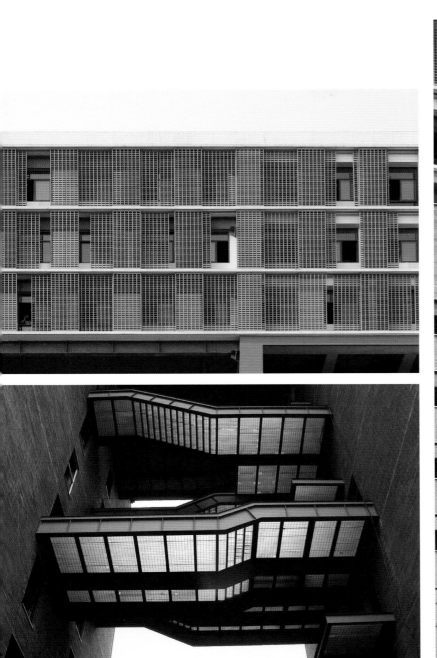

Left
The concave profile and tapered edge of the
building shifts its mass away from the neighbouring
tower block.

Opposite
An aerial rendering illustrates the rotated form of
the headquarters building in relation to the site's
existing components and open views.

An atrium runs continuously up through the office
floors, bringing daylight and lush planting as well
as natural ventilation to the internal environment.

JIE FANG DAILY NEWS HEADQUARTERS, HENAN ROAD, SHANGHAI

KAPLAN MCLAUGHLIN DIAZ, 2003–07

Jie Fang Daily News & Media Group (JFD) is the publisher of one of China's most influential newspapers. The expansion of its headquarters will accommodate the company's rapidly growing East China division. On a narrow site bounded by Henan Road and the existing JFD Tower, the proposed building partly defines the western edge of the historic Bund district, with unobstructed views east towards the Huangpu River and Pudong.

The architectural goal is to provide a state-of-the-art facility that encourages and facilitates interaction, integration and innovation among users, both inside and outside the organization. An environmentally sensitive development strategy addresses both the community's desire for a quality environment and JFD's functional needs in terms of future growth. The architects have developed an unusual 'double-green' approach, incorporating sustainable architecture to promote environmental responsibility while enhancing the users' relationship with ecology through natural spaces.

Through its rotation and concave façade, the majority of the building's mass is shifted to the east, away from the existing JFD Tower and creating a balanced composition with its neighbour. Simultaneously, its alignment with the prevailing south-easterly and north-easterly winds and its aerodynamic building form reduce wind loads on the structure and deflect wind away from pedestrians.

The transparent/translucent skin system and crystal sail-like character is intended to express JFD's leadership, objectivity and openness. The 'intelligent' curtain-wall system is embedded with light shelves and sunshading devices. The office floorplates, 18.3 metres at their widest, enjoy optimum daylight while suffering minimal solar gain. With traditional core components located on the west, most of the offices face directly east, enjoying panoramic views.

A glass atrium, or solarium, overflowing with planting, runs along the south-east edge of the building from bottom to top, connecting every floor of office space with a rooftop sky-garden. A stack effect is produced as hot air rises and gets vented from the top, drawing stale air from the office interiors into the atrium, where it is 'scrubbed' by trees as it ascends. Large volumes of fresh air are drawn into each floor through louvres on the opposite side of the building. This 'breathing effect' not only minimizes energy consumption but also makes the floorplates more efficient by reducing the capacity of the exhaust/ventilation system needed.

JIUSHI HEADQUARTERS, PUDONG, SHANGHAI

FOSTER AND PARTNERS, 1995–2001

The first major commercial building in Shanghai to be designed by a Western architect, the Jiushi Headquarters tower is located to the south of the famed Bund district, with views across the Huangpu River, and opposite the new business centre of Pudong. The forty-storey structure set a new benchmark for new building in the city, particularly in regard to environmental standards.

Foster and Partners' strategy was to provide a world-class building that could be realized largely by local means. The result is a simple, elegant structure, built to the highest specifications and orientated to capitalize on the attributes of its exceptional site. In response to the spectacular views, the building's service and circulation core is positioned away from the Huangpu River. This makes possible the creation of an open, flexible floorplate without internal columns, with panoramic views across the Bund and Pudong.

As the tower rises, its floorplates are stepped back from the envelope at three intervals to form sky-gardens that arch dramatically across the façade. This

culminates in a six-storey sky-garden at the top of the building, a surprising conclusion in a city where the roofs of towers typically accommodate service installations. The void creates a dramatic penthouse space as a backdrop to Jiushi Corporation's own offices.

The pure transparency of the tower's skin masks a sophisticated triple-glazing system that incorporates automatically controlled natural ventilation and allows maximum light penetration without solar gain in the office spaces.

A collaborative effort, using expertise from the UK, Japan and China, ensured that the project was completed to international standards, yet it is clearly rooted in its context and is sensitive to local architectural traditions. These traditions are particularly legible at street level, where a six-storey block at the base of the tower accommodates shops, restaurants and bars. The block follows the line of the street and incorporates a double-height colonnade that evokes nineteenth-century Shanghai shopping arcades.

Right
The Jiushi Headquarters tower, viewed from across the Huangpu River at night, is built on an exceptional site, with views across the historic Bund district.

Internal sky-gardens have been created along the edge of the tower.

Opposite
A night view of the tower illustrates how, at ground level, the building adopts the street scale and form with shops and restaurants.

LAN HUA INTERNATIONAL BUILDING, BEIJING

LEIGH & ORANGE, 2001–05

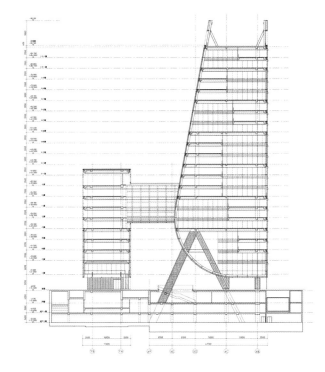

The Lan Hua International Building is a representative of a new generation of commercial architecture that is redefining Beijing. The development comprises two structures, one mirroring the other but at a different scale; it is primarily designed for office accommodation, but with entertainment and commercial uses enlivening the bridge between the two buildings.

Hong Kong-based practice Leigh & Orange has juxtaposed the two structures as a response to the site's context. The orientation takes account of the busy traffic junction, creating a landscaped plaza for the wider community that is secluded and identifiable as a civic place. Positioning was also determined by the insertion of vast atrium spaces extending the full height of the northernmost section in both buildings.

At the southern end of the site the two buildings stretch across to each other. Assembled around the link bridge are shared facilities such as conference rooms and meeting suites, and there is a café on the second floor of the baby structure. The physical joining of the two buildings is a poetic expression of bonding – parent and child embracing – and the congregation of social spaces across these arms reinforces the relationship. Clear glazing applied in rectangular panels lends the façades dynamic movement; the distinctive profiles of these panels are emphasized by the entwining ribbons of glass.

The forms of the buildings are not the results of whimsy. As they rise, their girth expanding then shrinking, the varying floorplate sizes and configurations fulfil the client's need for a choice of dimensions to suit different tenants. The horizontal and vertical layering shifts from one floor plane to the next, creating solid and void compositions that can be experienced from without and within.

Right
A section and rendering highlight the link bridge that unites the structures.

Opposite
A rendering of the illuminated development at night reveals the vertical and horizontal planes of the interiors.

NINGBO Y-TOWN, NINGBO

MADA S.P.A.M., 2002–04

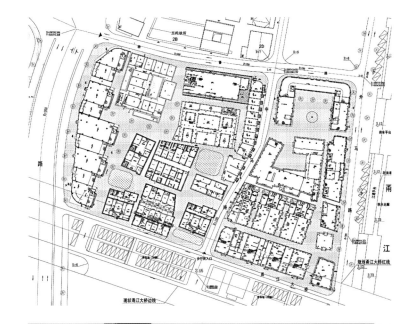

This commercial and retail project occupies a site that is often referred to as the Old Bund. MADA s.p.a.m. was asked to masterplan and design a dense, small-scale development with mixed commercial areas and a museum. Y-town presented the architects with an inherently contradictory proposition. Ningbo's urban condition has consistently been a primary concern to the team, yet the project's means of resolution lies outside the usual scope of its work. The area's classification as an historic district added a dimension to the brief – preservation – that MADA would normally avoid. However, the creative opportunities that history provides had the potential to produce a special result. The fragmented collaboration between the many industries involved in the project made the design and construction process extremely delicate, yet the aggregation of many types of knowledge became an invaluable resource.

These contradictions determined MADA's involvement with the processes of research, strategy-building, masterplanning, architectural design and interior design for the entire project. As it was difficult to arrive at independent and firm conclusions, the methodology became a process of establishing connecting points. In its role as moderator, the team had to develop a precise series of strategies that could bridge opposite poles of thought. Challenges included how to preserve the site's origins as an historic urban neighbourhood while also re-presenting it, rebuilding its original fabric yet introducing something new.

In defining the parameters, the design approach remained close to the specific site conditions. It was necessary to avoid the danger of over-precision, so the development extracts its programmatic organization and spatial configuration from the urban environment. The resulting intricacies and complexity serve to enrich the project's experience for users.

Right
The site plan marks the clear boundaries between the highway, bridge and river.

A preserved chimney reveals the site's industrial nature.

Opposite
Paved streets weave their way through the development.

A bird's-eye view shows the historic urban neighbourhood in context.

Buildings are juxtaposed along the roadside edge of the complex.

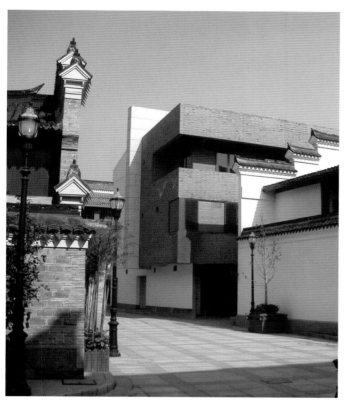

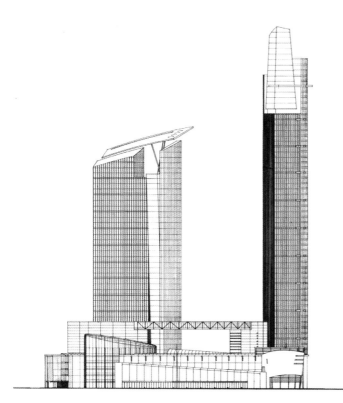

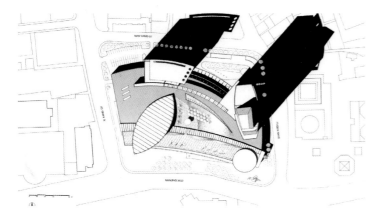

PLAZA 66, NANJING XI LU, SHANGHAI

KOHN PEDERSEN FOX ASSOCIATES, 1994–2001

Located in the heart of old Shanghai, the site occupies a pivotal position within the city's downtown shopping district. KPF was asked by the Hang Lung Development Company to design a complex that combines two office towers – one sixty-storey, the other forty-storey – with a major retail mall. The commission, undertaken in association with Frank C.Y. Feng Architects and Associates (HK), posed several major challenges. Arguably the foremost of these was the need to mediate between the popular pedestrian thoroughfare of Nanjing Xi Lu and the enormous size of the buildings.

The programme incorporates a mix of retail, entertainment and extensive underground parking areas with more than 93,000 square metres of office space in Tower I and 90,000 square metres in the proposed Tower II. Addressing the two opposing scales, KPF's solution was to devise a series of radially inspired volumes in the form of a lozenge, cone, almond and arc, and collage them on the site. The four

entities are bound together by a five-storey retail podium; however, each component clearly retains its formal independence.

The volumes are distinguished by a canted feature in the form of a sectional tilt or cut, which establishes separate entry sequences as it meets the ground. Closer to street level, these elements conform to the human scale of the neighbourhood's historic structures and contribute to the busy street life of Nanjing Xi Lu. With a podium containing more than 50,000 square metres of retail space, the shopping experience is punctuated by two major interior public atriums. Wrapped by curved volumes, these two voids are embraced by the tower walls.

From outside, the spiralling masses of the towers give an impression of skyward movement, as if they were caught up in a vortex. The eye is drawn up, ascending some 281 metres to the pinnacle of Tower I to rest on a lantern structure made from glass screens. When illuminated at night, it is visible from all directions.

Opposite

Night-time illumination distinguishes the different volumes of the complex.

A detail highlights the juxtaposition of various materials.

The skylit atrium enhances the shopping experience.

Above

An elevation and aerial perspective reveal the intricate relationship between the functional components.

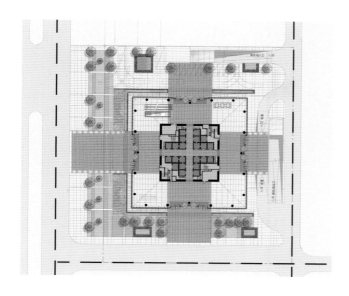

R&F CENTRE, GUANGZHOU

AEDAS, 2003–05

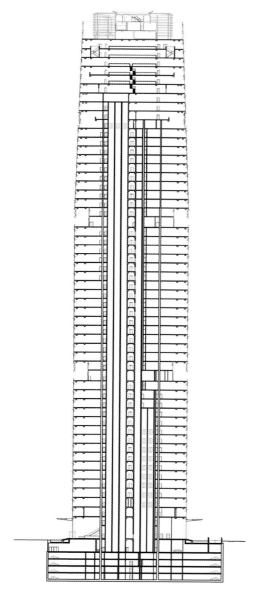

With a prime location among a growing number of tall towers in Guangzhou's burgeoning Central Business District (CBD), R&F Centre sets a benchmark for the city's skyscrapers. The owner, Guangzhou R&F Properties Group, commissioned Aedas to design a 200-metre super high-rise that would be an icon for Guangzhou, reinforcing its identity and providing a monumental landmark on the banks of the Pearl River.

The top ten floors of the fifty-four-storey commercial office tower are reserved for the developer's headquarters. With a gross floor area of 121,755 square metres and a footprint of 8117 square metres, the building is designed to use space with great efficiency. However, its design concept derives from the sculptural forms of China's historic jade vases. It also conforms symbolically to the Chinese philosophy of architecture and space: hence, at ground level the building is square, signifying formality and elegance. Surrounded by a green, landscaped plaza, the entrance is marked by a triple-height lobby space. An elegant canopy protrudes from the outer edge, encircling the tower and

protecting users from the weather.

The tower is defined as a singular, fluid entity in transparent glass. A lighting feature on the curtain wall reflects the image of a white jade vase. Low-e glass and external sunshading devices are used in preference to reflective glass in China because of the need to mitigate solar gain and save energy on air-conditioning. On the eighteenth and thirty-fifth floors the corners of the elevation are scooped out to create sky-terraces. These are shaded from the glaring sun by louvre-style screens. Higher up, the headquarters lobby marks the forty-fifth level.

A tight central lift core maximizes the open-plan column-free work spaces with typical floor areas of 2400 square metres, giving tenants ample flexibility. A subtle kink in the tower's elevation indicates the front of the building, and this is illuminated at night, emphasizing the structure's rising form. The stretched perspective is also heightened by the tower's gently tapering plan, which draws the building to a conclusion at the top by extending the inner core of the structure upwards.

Opposite
The iconic profile of the office tower is matched by crisply articulated lobby spaces and core details.

Left
Drawings show the landscaped plaza surrounding the tower and its composite section.

SHANGHAI WORLD FINANCIAL CENTER, PUDONG, SHANGHAI

KOHN PEDERSEN FOX ASSOCIATES, 1993-2007

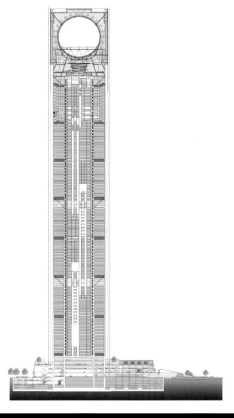

When completed, the Shanghai World Financial Center will be the tallest building in the world at 492 metres. Its prominent site lies in the Lujiazhui financial and trade district in Pudong, a key area designated by the Chinese government as a centre for international banking and commerce. Uninhibited and rapid development in this part of the city has produced an urban fabric that is often fragmented and unengaging. The architects have responded with a design that radiates monolithic simplicity.

The programme of this 101-storey mixed-use development falls into two distinctly formal components – a sculpted tower and a podium – incorporating offices, a 300-room luxury hotel, retail facilities, gallery and observation deck.

Designed in association with Mori Building Architects & Engineers and the East China Architectural Design & Research Institute, the 333,500-square-metre project relates to its context through an abstract language that incorporates characteristics that have meaning within Chinese architectural tradition. The form of the tower corresponds to a fundamental Chinese concept that perceives the earth as a square and the sky as a circle. The interaction of these two geometric elements gives the skyscraper its identifiable image while also relating to its context. The tower is primarily a square prism intersected by two sweeping arcs that gradually taper into a flattened, single line at the apex. Rather than a whimsical gesture, the form fulfils an essential requirement of the brief. The succession of different-sized floorplates generates configurations that are ideal for offices on the lower floors and hotel suites above.

As the plan evolves, the upper portion of the tower is rotated towards the nearby Oriental Pearl TV Tower, a dominant landmark on Shanghai's skyline. To relieve wind pressure, a 50-metre cylinder, matching the diameter of the sphere of the television tower, is punched out of the top of the building. In this respect, the void attempts to connect the two structures visually across the urban landscape. Towards street level, smaller geometric forms, complementing those of the tower, penetrate its massive stone base, providing a sense of human scale while organizing pedestrian circulation around the point of entry.

Right
A section through the tower and an aerial view of the model emphasize the simplicity of the skyscraper.

Opposite
Different perspectives of the tower's form illustrate how its square base tapers as it rises into a single line.

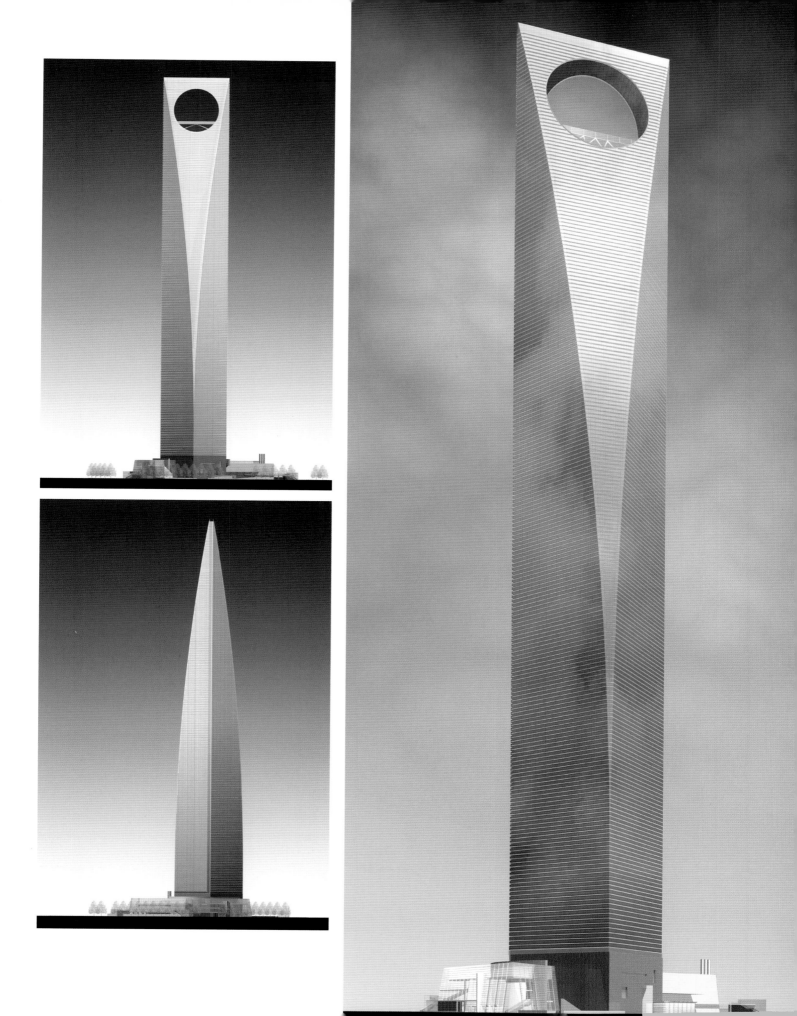

SHENZHEN URBAN-PLANNING BUREAU OFFICE, SHENZHEN

URBANUS ARCHITECTURE AND DESIGN, 2001–04

Shenzhen has experienced rapid urbanization over the last twenty years, growing from a tiny fishing village to today's metropolis of six million inhabitants. In many ways, Shenzhen is the generic Asian city where history and cultural heritage have been swept aside in the quest for fast economic growth.

Urbanus takes this context into consideration in the design of 28,000-square-metre offices for the Shenzhen Urban-Planning Bureau. Its compact form has a simple but expressive silhouette, in contrast to the anonymity of the surroundings. The client's various requirements included exhibition spaces, conference facilities and office accommodation. The building responds with various degrees of transparency: functions are clearly organized in relation to the glazed façade so that they are apparent to outsiders.

The glass façade is articulated in horizontal bands, stretching the perspective and reflecting the changing seasons of the natural landscape. Unlike the rigidly imposing architecture of typical government buildings, this development is a statement of openness, transparency and modesty. The architects have balanced this aesthetic with a minimal and restrained composition

that presents the serious, business-like face appropriate to government bodies. The unorthodox treatment also applies to the intimate connection that the building makes with the ground plane: the two are barely discernible as separate elements, so the structure becomes an extension of its surroundings.

Access to the building is across bridges that cross shallow ponds, creating a poetic relationship and simultaneously addressing security concerns. Internally, the wide application of glass is also evident in the transparent spatial organization of the interlocking parts. The design introduces sustainable principles with the use of dual-level units that are conceived as the basic modular cells of the office system. Built within a lightweight steel framework, the components can expand when and if programmatic needs change. Thus flexibility is built into the system, and changes can be accommodated without disruption.

Several atriums behind the glass wall serve as transition zones and buffers against the hot climate. The voids are cooled by evaporation and natural convection; hot air escapes through vents in the roof, and fresh air drawn across the atriums is cooled by ponds.

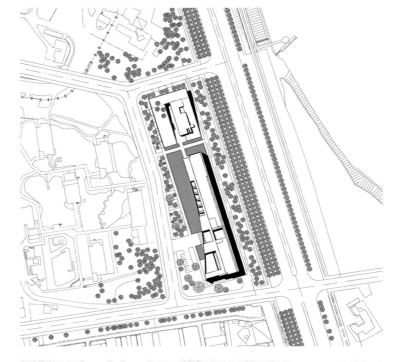

Right
The site plan and building model highlight the linearity of the architecture.

Opposite
The building's horizontal façade articulation gives way to a transparent organization of spatial layers.

SHOPPING YARD, LANGFANG CITY, HEBEI

JINAO KANN FINCH DESIGN GROUP, 2000–02

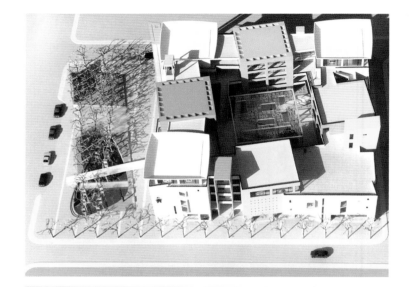

A successful shopping mall must have as much street frontage as possible in order to engage passers-by. At Shopping Yard, a mall with a floor area of 13,000 square metres, a grid outlines a square footprint totalling 60 × 60 metres – two streets on an east–west alignment and two aligned north to south. This breaks the building mass down into nine pavilions, all of which embrace a central courtyard, increasing the visibility of each unit.

Stores vary both by size and merchandise, ranging from department stores and supermarkets to franchised boutiques and restaurants/cafés. The street concept is applied to all the floors of the centre, and each is themed in a different manner to enrich the experience of shopping. Colour coding further maps out the individual structures, helping to orient users while distinguishing particular features of the façades.

Fifth Street is considered as a commercial realm, running for 70 metres from north to south. It forms a transitional intersection with the classical Western architectural character of First Street. First Street is understood as a prelude to Sixth Street, which features a mall shopping centre with individual shops and restaurants.

The height of each block corresponds to adjacent buildings and varies from three to five storeys. The four corner blocks neatly enclose the site and are denoted in white to set out the parameter of the mall, while inviting exploration. Attention to the immediate context is also considered in the scale and colour tones of the other buildings. Visibility is increased vertically through the use of trellised walkways, open arcades and perforated walls, giving the impression that the architecture is easily penetrable.

Right
An aerial view of the model depicts the nine pavilions that make up the shopping centre.

Semi-shaded circulation paths promote visibility around the central courtyard.

Opposite
The two different street-side façades are treated according to the scale and form of the surroundings.

Colour coding helps to identify different retail elements.

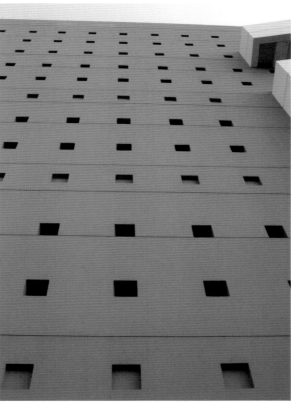

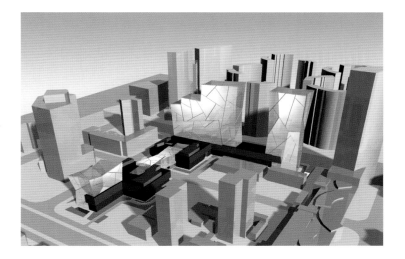

SOHO SHANG DU, DONGDAQIAO LU, BEIJING
LAB ARCHITECTURE STUDIO, 2004–07

Opposite
A rendering of the faceted tower forms emphasizes their intricate façade design.

Above and below
Experienced in its urban context, the parametric geometry of the towers creates a changing perspective of the site.

This 170,000-square-metre mixed-use development will occupy 22 hectares of a special development zone in the heart of Beijing's Central Business District. The Shang Du towers are designed as crystalline forms with faceted surfaces that are embedded into a horizontal base of retail blocks. The main towers are designated for residential, studio and office use. Together, they will constitute a distinctive urban marker on Dongdaqiao Lu. The façade design and, particularly, the format of the night lighting give the complex a distinctive profile against the city skyline. The pattern and light lines inscribed on the tower surface are inspired by a parametric geometry that relates to the 'ice-ray' designs found on traditional Chinese wooden screens.

Developed as high-rise 'warehouse shells', the two main towers allow a variety of functional occupations and size configurations. The surface geometry generates variable floorplates, ranging from 75 to 600 square metres, which the client can use to match unit sizes to demand. A series of 'loft' units, to which internal mezzanines can be added, have been integrated into the development. So that they can be adapted for retail use, they are positioned in the lower levels of the main north and south towers, immediately above the retail block, where they are given high window frontages on the main street.

The retail component has evolved from a design that links the two sides of the site. Conceived as an aggregate of filaments bundled together and tied in the middle,

corresponding with the bridge, its sections change both vertically and horizontally, creating a variety of experiences between intimacy and openness. On either side of the bridge, the five floors of the retail blocks form an irregular network of lanes providing access to all corners of the plan without any dead ends or backtracking.

The visual liveliness of the public spaces is intensified inside – an idea based on the analogy of a geode, a rock with a deceptively simple exterior, which, when cut, reveals an extraordinary crystalline interior. Animated by these multifaceted surfaces, the experience of promenading through the space, with its simultaneous perspectives and dramatic vertical sightlines, generates much of the mall's theatrical charm.

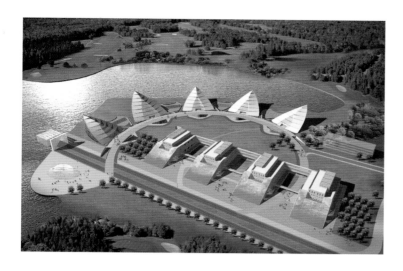

SONGSANGHU CITY HOUSE, DONGGUAN, GUANGDONG

QIXIN ARCHITECTS AND ENGINEERS, 2002–05

Opposite
Viewed from across the lake, the triangular buildings maximize the length of their water frontages.

From the central plaza there are open views across the site.

Above
An aerial rendering of the site shows the radiating disposition of buildings.

Below
Internally, the architecture makes the most of its openness, both vertical and horizontal.

Sited on a peninsula almost surrounded by water, this office development enjoys stunning open views and a close relationship with the natural environment. Qixin Architects and Engineers capitalize on the site's attributes in the orientation of the building components. Facing south-west towards the water and bordered by two roads to the north and east, the development has been conceived in conjunction with plans to build a convention centre and a five-star hotel towards the eastern end of the site.

The primary concern of the architects was to avoid major disruption to the environment. In terms of accommodation, the brief did not demand a great deal of floor area. Using the largely flat and gently sloping topography of the site, the project is fragmented into a complex of smaller buildings, leaving a large central green oasis with ample sunlight and open views towards the lake.

The constellation of structures is organized logically, with the exhibition centre and smaller office buildings located to the east, close to the public areas. Another

cluster of buildings spans the south of the site, closer to the lake. In order to make the most of the views, the structures are designed with a triangular plan, doubling the frontage facing the water.

The five triangular buildings are linked to a circular carpark at lower-ground level. A strip of independent office buildings linked to the exhibition centre runs along the main road. The development forms a holistic arrangement in which the building masses are scattered and integrated with the existing environment.

THREE ON THE BUND, SHANGHAI

MICHAEL GRAVES & ASSOCIATES, 2001–04

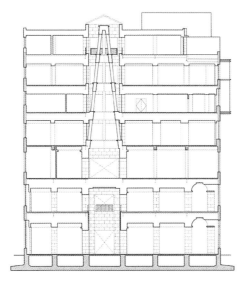

Located in Shanghai's historic Bund quarter along the Huangpu River, the project called for the comprehensive remodelling of a seven-storey historic structure built in 1916 for the Union Assurance Company. Michael Graves & Associates was commissioned as design architect for the public spaces and selected restaurants. While the Neo-classical exterior of the Beaux-Arts building has been meticulously restored to its former glory, the interior has been completely transformed. It is now a modern destination for art, shopping, dining and leisure.

Combining 12,422 square metres of floor area with ceiling heights averaging more than 5 metres, the building is functionally zoned: retail stores and art galleries occupy the first three floors, while exclusive dining venues take up the higher levels, along with a café, music club, spa and roof terrace. The architect has preserved many of the building's original features, including the fireplaces in the main lobby, now restored and relocated, and the cornices on the third floor. Materials have been carefully considered and underline the status and character of the development as well as its context; they include Douglas fir,

cippolino verde marble, bamboo plank, tempered glass, and 'Riverstone', an Italian product comprising marble pebbles suspended in clear epoxy resin.

Arguably the most striking aspects of the interior also remain intact – the west and east atriums – although both have been dramatically redesigned. The intention was to create a more open, public environment by reconfiguring the internal circulation and inserting a grand skylit central stair. The walls of the east atrium are clad in translucent alabaster, projecting a veil of light through the building. The full-height atriums are essential to promoting vertical orientation and connectivity. With shafts of daylight seeping down to all the floors, the inwardly tilting walls and rounded columns supported by piers of intricately figured green marble create a vertical landscape alluding to a mountain forest.

The language of the three vertical elements – the two atriums and the staircase – is continued beyond the roofline, forming lanterns to the sky and blending with the small structures that appear on other typical Bund buildings.

Opposite
Interior dining and entertainment spaces occupy the upper floors of the building.

There are two full-height atriums, providing vertical orientation and natural light to users.

Left
A section reveals the complex configurations of the internal spaces.

The historic building faces Shanghai's renowned Bund.

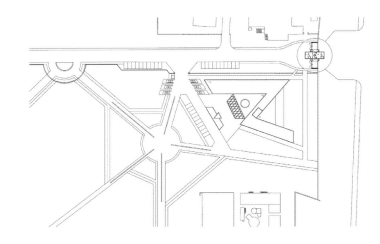

TIANJIN HUASHI OFFICE BUILDING, TIANJIN DAGANG POWER PLANT, TIANJIN

XWG (BEIJING TSINGHUA ARCHITECTURAL DESIGN & CONSULTATION), 2001–03

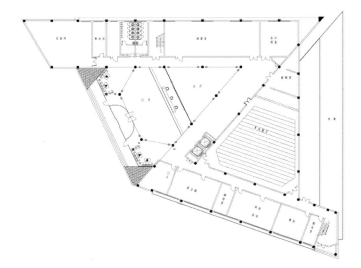

The Tianjin Huashi Company's office building is situated to the north-east of the Tianjin Dagang Power Plant. Its two-dimensional profile is both a result of the limitations imposed by the surrounding roads and buildings and a metaphor expressing the specific function of the power plant – in plan it resembles the warning sign for electricity. The main entrance to the office building faces south-west, opposite the plant's central square and linked to the main generator room.

The five-storey block has an N-shaped plan containing the offices of all the departments that support the power plant. This framework creates two large openings. On one side the space is allocated to a large lecture hall and convention room, while the other side is left as a void connecting to the main lobby. This multistorey void identifies the heart of the building, its significance heightened by its role as a space connector and organizer,

linking up all the offices in every direction. The aperture also serves as an air tube, drawing fresh air up to all the office spaces.

The building is clad where possible in transparent glazing, bringing ample natural light into the entrance lobby, the multistorey void and the break-out foyer on the east side of the lecture hall. Circulation spaces on the periphery also help access to light and open views. The suspended roof structure provides the opportunity for open terraces on the fifth floor. Circular cut-outs in the roof let the sky peep through. The glass curtain is a double-glazed unit comprising two six-layered panels of glass.

In its zig-zagging composition, the form of the building signals the nature of the company's business. Its transparency is an indication of how the company conducts that business. Through the glass curtain, the clarity of the post-and-beam structure, the suspended ceiling and the overhanging floor slab make a harmonious composition.

Right
The site and floor plans reveal the N-shaped configuration of the office building, which accommodates a multistorey void.

Opposite
The office building, shown from west and south views, expresses a strong corporate image with its energetic dynamics.

There are open views across the site from the fifth-floor terrace.

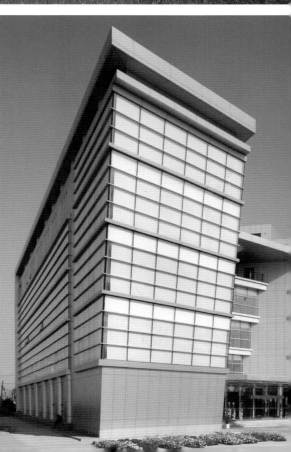

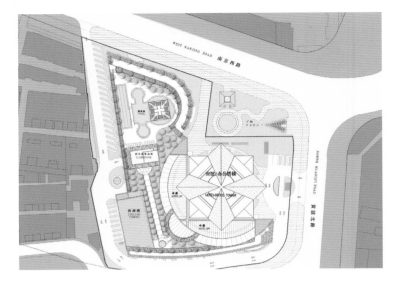

TOMORROW SQUARE, SHANGHAI

JOHN PORTMAN & ASSOCIATES, 1996–2002

Tomorrow Square occupies a prominent site at the top end of Nanjing Road, one of Shanghai's most popular shopping destinations. John Portman & Associates wanted to create a distinctive and prestigious complex that would be economically viable but also herald the twenty-first century in terms of state-of-the-art building technology. The basic intention was to provide a multifunctional commercial and residential development that would greatly enhance the quality of urban living for its inhabitants and users.

The complex programme initially called for hotel accommodation, offices, retail and restaurant facilities, entertainment amenities – including a night club, spa, bowling lanes, indoor golf, tennis court and swimming pool – and conference/meeting spaces. After the shell was constructed it was decided that the offices should be converted to serviced apartments, a decision that tested the design's inherent flexibility even before the building was complete.

Tomorrow Square is close to People's Square and People's Park, two of Shanghai's most important civic spaces, and the building's design embraces both.

The three major elements – high-rise hotel and serviced-apartment tower, atrium and low-rise podium – are planted on a landscaped plaza. The first thirty-six floors of the sixty-storey tower rise vertically. Above them, the tower's plan is rotated 45 degrees to optimize views for hotel guests and park visitors. Aluminium and glass clad the tower, angled to accentuate the upward thrusting of the form.

Accommodation within the tower comprises 255 executive apartments topped by a J.W. Marriott Hotel. The hotel's 342 guestrooms are divided between deluxe rooms measuring 38 square metres, and executive suites that measure 66–82 square metres. A large food court, entertainment and shopping centre occupy the six-storey atrium, which is flooded with natural light. This 18,580-square-metre granite podium base also contains 1300 square metres of business and health facilities.

Tomorrow Square's distinctive profile adds flair to the city's downtown shopping hub, creating a new axial point that orientates pedestrians and traffic.

Right
The site plan describes the components of the complex and its prominent location.

A section reveals the elements of the development: a low-rise podium, a tower comprising apartments and a hotel, and an atrium.

Opposite
The distinctive articulation and detail are highlights of the soaring tower.

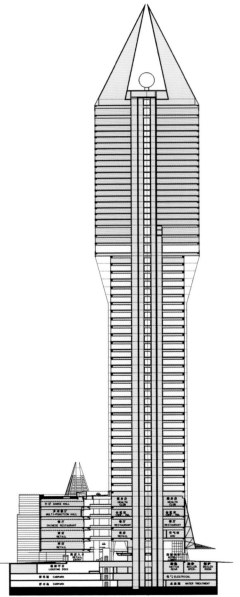

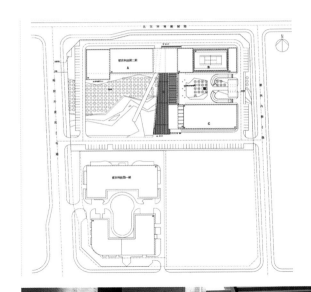

WANGJING SCIENCE & TECHNOLOGY CAMPUS – SECOND PHASE, WANGJING, BEIJING

BEIJING INSTITUTE OF ARCHITECTURAL DESIGN, 2000–04

Located on the edge of the city, where building densities are substantially lower than they are closer to the centre, the second phase of the Wangjing Science & Technology Campus involved the design of a series of office buildings to support the educational institution. The architects took advantage of the lower plot ratio and the more open environment of the 2.6-hectare site. As is usual in Beijing, the building follows the site boundary, maintaining a sense of order and formality. It opens into a landscaped square to the north, where it meets the first phase of the project. Embraced by the sequence of buildings, the green open space brings the whole complex together as one entity.

With a total floor area of 46,000 square metres, the second-phase accommodation is divided between three buildings with one connecting corridor providing access to the various departments. While each has particular functions, the individual structures are assembled into a coherent whole, playing off each other with their respective orientations and forming an intricate series of relationships. Similar treatments define the external articulation.

Two of the buildings lie towards the north, aligned along the same axis. A connecting block feeds into the third building on the southern edge of the site. Inside, there are lobbies, cafés, exhibition areas and office spaces. The block also channels users into the main entrance to one of the buildings, via a staircase to the second floor.

The two main volumes resemble upturned rectangles along a folded line. The other is U-shaped and clad in highly reflective glass. Structures with various forms protrude across each other and overhang the landscaped plaza, reinforcing the three-way dialogue of the complex. Larger spaces in the six-storey blocks are reserved for functions such as the conference centre and gymnasium.

Right
The site plan shows the new complex in relation to the existing buildings.

The connecting block feeds into the various components, serving as a circulation corridor but also accommodating communal facilities.

Opposite
Intersecting and overhanging volumes create an intricate set of relationships between the three blocks.

The north side of the complex faces a landscaped plaza.

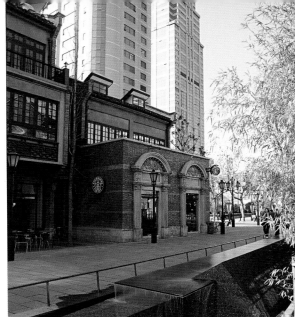

XINTIANDI, SHANGHAI

WOOD AND ZAPATA, 1998–2001

This project involved the restoration, renovation and new construction of two city blocks in a historic French Concession (Longtang) area of Shanghai. Responsibility for transforming the neighbourhood into a buzzing commercial and residential district was taken on by architectural and urban-planning firm Wood and Zapata. Its design successfully marries traditional and ultra-modern architecture in a format that is intensely vibrant, vehicle-free and humanly scaled. Since its completion, Xintiandi has become one of the city's most popular shopping, leisure and dining destinations. The mixture of uses manages to preserve the authenticity of the original *shikumen* houses, remaining culturally sensitive to the area's history, while the insertion of new structures lends the area a much-needed feeling of contemporaneity.

The site is anchored by two main features: the First Congress Building and the central plaza. The First Congress Building is a former residence that was the Chinese Communist Party's first meeting place. It now combines retail, cultural, recreational and commercial activities.

The central plaza was created with lush landscaping, outdoor cafés, fountains and show areas, providing places in which visitors can linger. Secondary alleyways meander around and feed into the main square, contributing to the area's diversity and charm, while promoting the experience of discovery and surprise.

The *shikumen* buildings that previously crammed the crowded lanes of Xintiandi dated from the early twentieth century, their style reflecting a combination of influences from home and abroad. Today, the central open space known as Xintiandi Plaza is considered an important Shanghai landmark, covering 30,000 square metres with a gross floor area extending to 60,000 square metres. Wood and Zapata has meticulously preserved the brickwork structures, cobbled streets and decorative tiling to evoke the ambience of 1920s Shanghai. The remodelling has extended the life of this historic quarter – now occupied by stylish boutiques, gourmet dining spots and contemporary art galleries – in a manner that parallels Shanghai's increasingly cosmopolitan lifestyle.

Opposite
An intricate network of outdoor spaces and pathways enlivens the development.

Left
The site plan details the street layout.

New architectural additions create an intriguing blend of modern and traditional.

YIN TAI CENTRE, BEIJING

JOHN PORTMAN & ASSOCIATES, 2001–07

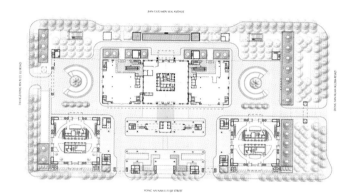

This commercial and residential development will add a distinctive element to the city's skyline. Its underlying highlight is a luscious waterpark that forms a landscaped base to the three towers.

Square in form and clearly articulated, twin 45-storey office blocks flank a 62-storey hotel tower, cleverly reflecting each other's bold geometry. Sky-lobbies are inserted into the office towers, effectively slicing each vertically to enable the buildings to work as four independent units. The hotel component – with 550 guestrooms and 150 serviced apartments – has a symbol added to its profile. The top of the rectilinear tower is treated subtly differently, a large latticed light cube – which can be interpreted as a Chinese lantern – crowning the building. At night it becomes a beacon, projecting light across the city to announce its presence.

A podium anchors the three blocks at ground level and provides a point of connection. It contains lobbies, meeting facilities, shops and restaurants. The architecture does not end with the podium.

Underneath it, vehicles coming into the site enter monumental spaces that provide a grand sense of an entrance to each tower. The roof of the podium is conceived as an urban park and an extension of the gardens at street level, together forming a lushly planted multilevel landscape that creates an intimate, human-scaled encounter with nature. Strategically placed water features help to separate this environment from the heavy traffic that encircles the site.

Yin Tai Centre combines many of the components that the Portman practice considers essential to architecture, its humanist concern and programmatic requirements tied to a form that is sensitive to cultural and contextual parameters. By integrating large and small spaces and weaving nature into the architecture, Portman creates sensory appeal. His view of what defines indigenous forms in new architecture is conveyed by the way Yin Tai Centre provides a bridge to the past while also reflecting the spirit of its creation.

Opposite
The three towers are anchored at ground level by a podium that houses restaurants, shops and meeting facilities.

Left
The site plan outlines the waterpark that forms a landscaped base to the towers.

The interior lobbies and meeting areas are characterized by double-height volumes that emphasize space and light.

ZHONG GUANCUN WEST, HAI DIAN, BEIJING

KOHN PEDERSEN FOX ASSOCIATES, 2002–05

Zhong Guancun West is the tallest and most centrally located development in the district. Designed by KPF with associate architect China Architectural Design and Research Institute, the client, Beijing Science & Technology Park, asked for a mixed-use facility with offices, a technology centre, residential accommodation, retail amenities, a hotel and convention/exhibition space.

The masterplan takes the form of an arc of a circle, with the building designated to its curved edge. KPF also took into account the two parks that flank the complex. Their presence enhances the development's monumentality as well as providing views and landscaped open space.

Comprising a total of 95,000 square metres above ground, Zhong Guancun West comprises an office tower with a podium and an exhibition structure bridging them in a curving gesture that mirrors the crescent shape of the plan. It embraces the two parks by generously framing vistas to both. The bridge flanks the thirty-five-storey office tower to the north and the podium to the south, providing both a striking connection between them and an identifiable gateway to the complex.

The architecture is conceived as a series of curved planes and volumes, in glass and metal. Its composition provides an image of technology as dynamic and forward-looking. The profile of the office tower is gently tapered at either end, and its form is articulated as two interlocking segments.

While each volume is intended to express the purpose of what takes place inside, the technical specifications of Zhong Guancun West define the highest level of building practice in Beijing. The development's position provides the benefits of proximity to other buildings and services, but the complex itself will become an icon for the future of technology in China.

e era

Opposite
An aerial view of the model and exterior renderings depict the exhibition building that links the office tower and the podium. Its arched form reflects the nature of the site.

Left
Lofty ceilings and full-height glazing characterize the interior spaces.

FURTHER READING

Books

Chan, Bernard, *Athletic Facilities, One Hundred Outstanding Architects,* Hong Kong (Pace Publishing Ltd) 2002

Chan, Bernard, *Commercial Buildings, One Hundred Outstanding Architects*, Hong Kong (Pace Publishing Ltd) 2002

Chan, Bernard, *Educational Facilities, One Hundred Outstanding Architects*, Hong Kong (Pace Publishing Ltd) 2002

Chan, Bernard, *Gateways, One Hundred Outstanding Architects*, Hong Kong (Pace Publishing Ltd) 2002

Cody, Jeffrey, *Building in China – Henry K. Murphy's Adaptive Architecture, 1914–1935*, Hong Kong (Chinese University Press) 2001

Gutierrez, Laurent, and Portefaix, Valerie, *Yung Ho Chang: Atelier Feichang Jianzhu – A Chinese Practice*, Hong Kong (Map Book Publishers) 2003

Kögel, Eduard, and Meyer, Ulf, *The Chinese City: Between Tradition and Modernism*, Berlin (Jovis Verlag) 2000

Liu, Erming, and Yi, Feng (eds.), *Chinese Architecture Since 1980: Memories and Solutions of Young Architects*, Beijing (Encyclopedia of China Publishing House) 1997

Liu, Erming, *et al.*, *International Architects in China: Selected Works Since 1980*, Beijing (China Planning Press and Encyclopedia of China Publishing House) 1999

Vockler, Kai, and Luckow, Dirk (eds.), *Beijing, Shanghai, Shenzhen – Cities of the 21st Century*, Frankfurt (Campus Verlag) 2000

World Architecture Magazine Publication and Crystal Computer Graphics Company, *33 Young Chinese Architects*, Beijing (Intellectual Property Publishing House) 2001

Xue, Charlie Q.L., *Building a Revolution: Chinese Architecture Since 1980*, Hong Kong (Hong Kong University Press) 2005

Yim, Rocco, *Being Chinese in Architecture: Recent Works in China by Rocco Design*, Hong Kong (MCCM Creations) 2004

Zou, Denang, *Modern History of Chinese Architecture*, Beijing (China Building and Architectural Press) 2000

Articles

Miao, Pu, 'In the Absence of Authenticity – An Interpretation of Contemporary Chinese Architecture', *Nordisk Arkitekturforskning: Nordic Journal of Architectural Research*, vol. 8, no. 3, 1995

Xue, Charlie Q.L., 'Artistic Reflection in Contemporary Chinese Architecture', *Taasa Review: The Journal of the Asian Arts Society of Australia*, vol. 13, no. 4, December 2004

PICTURE CREDITS

The illustrations in this book have been reproduced courtesy of the following copyright holders:

Jacket, front: Satoshi Asakawa; jacket, back: John Butlin; Bi Kejian p. 2; Didier Boy de la Tour p. 6; Ellerbe Becket p. 8; Tomio Ohashi p. 9; Paul Maurer p. 10; Wong Da Gang p. 11; Shen Zhonghai p. 12; David Liu of IRP3 Ltd p. 13; Chen Jian Gang p. 14; Herzog & de Meuron p. 15; NBBJ pp. 18–19, 186–87; Fan Hong/Institute of Architecture Design & Research pp. 20–21; RTKL International pp. 22–23; Rocco Design pp. 24–25; Li Wen of Point Studio/Paul Andreu Architecte pp. 26–27; Zaha Hadid Architects pp. 28–29; Kohn Pedersen Fox Associates pp. 30–31, 188–89, 212–13, 234–35; Bi Kejian/Jiakun Architects pp. 32–33, 158–59; gmp – von Gerkan, Marg und Partner Architects pp. 34–35, 40–41, 62–63; Steven Holl Architects pp. 36–37, 108–109; Paul Andreu Architecte pp. 38–39; MADA s.p.a.m. pp. 42–43, 48–49, 120–21, 206–207; Sasaki Associates pp. 44–45; Shen Zhonghai/Paul Andreu Architecte pp. 46–47; Jörg Hempel/Tilke Engineers and Architects pp. 50–51; Tim Griffith/RTKL International pp. 52–53; Jamie Ardiles-Arce, Miao Zhi Jian/Sydness Architects pp. 54–55; Cox Richardson Architects & Planners pp. 56–57; Open Architecture pp. 58–59; Atelier Feichang Jianzhu pp. 60–61; AXS Satow pp. 64–65; Gao Hongqi/Studio Wang Lu pp. 66–67; PTW Architects and CSCEC-SDI pp. 68–69; Burckhardt+Partner pp. 70–71; Kisho Kurokawa Architect & Associates pp. 72–73; Foster and Partners pp. 76–77; Henn Architekten pp. 78–79; RMJM HK pp. 80–81, 112–113, 156–57, 194–95; PTW Architects pp. 82–83; Shinkenchiku-sha/AXS Satow pp. 84–85; Green Spring Media/Parsons/URS Greiner/Guangdong Provincial Architectural Design Institute pp. 86–87; Urbanus Architecture and Design pp. 88–89, 192–93; Jan Siefke/gmp – von Gerkan, Marg und Partner Architects pp. 90–91, 96–97; Fu Xing/Woodhead International pp. 92–93; Doug Snower, Chen Bairong, Miu Zhijang and Yang Quitao/Murphy/Jahn pp. 94–95; Zhang Guangyuan/China Architecture Design & Research Group pp. 98–99, 164–65; Satoshi Asakawa, Ma Xiaochun/Chien Hsueh-Yi pp. 102–103; Satoshi Asakawa/Kengo Kuma pp. 104–105; T.R. Hamzah & Yeang pp. 106–107; Tomio Ohashi, Ma Xiaochun/Rocco Yim and Seung H-Sang pp. 110–11; Satoshi Asakawa, Ma Xiaochun/ Antonio Ochoa-Piccardo pp. 114–15; Satoshi Asakawa, Ma Xiaochun/Rocco Yim pp. 116–17;

Kerun Ip/HOK International (Asia/Pacific) pp. 118–19; Satoshi Asakawa, Ma Xiaochun/ Shigeru Ban pp. 122–23; Satoshi Asakawa/Riken Yamamoto pp. 124–25; Satoshi Asakawa/Cui Kai pp. 126–27; Satoshi Asakawa/Kanika R'Kul pp. 128–29; Satoshi Asakawa, Ma Xiaochun/Yung Ho Chang pp. 130–31; Zhang Lei, Wang Kai/Atelier Zhanglei pp. 132–33; Ma Xiaochun/Fake Design pp. 134–35; Satoshi Asakawa, Ma Xiaochun/Gary Chang pp. 136–37; Zhang Siye/Atelier Deshaus pp. 138–39; Fu Xing/gmp – von Gerkan, Marg und Partner Architects pp. 140–41; Fu Xing/ Institute of Architecture Design & Research pp. 144–45, 162–63; Ma Xiaochun/XWG (Beijing Tsinghua Architectural Design & Consultation) pp.146–47; Zhang Siye, Liu Yichun/Atelier Deshaus pp. 148–49; Jan Siefke, Yang Chaoying/gmp – von Gerkan, Marg und Partner Architects pp. 150–51; Fu Xing, Fang Zhenning, Qi Xin/Jinao Kann Finch Design Group pp. 152–53, 216–17; KSP Engel und Zimmermann Architects pp. 154–55; Zhang Yanlai, Li Xiang/Luo Siwei pp. 160–61; Wang Shu, Lu Wenyu/Amateur Architecture Studio pp. 166–67; Zhu Jingxiang/Zhu Jingxiang Studio pp. 168–71; Kiyohiko Higashide, Kerun Ip/Pei Partnership Architects pp. 174–75; OMA pp. 176–77, 182–83; Zhang Siyi/Arquitectonica pp. 178–79; Michael Portman, Dai Weiping/John Portman & Associates pp. 180–81; Skidmore, Owings & Merrill pp. 184–85; Arquitectonica pp. 190–91; The Jerde Partnership pp. 196–97; Fu Xing/Atelier Feichang Jianzhu pp. 198–99; Kaplan McLaughlin Diaz pp. 200–201; Kerun Ip/Foster and Partners pp. 202–203; Leigh & Orange pp. 204–205; John Butlin/Kohn Pedersen Fox Associates pp. 208–209; Aedas pp. 210–11; Shu He, Wu Tong/Urbanus Architecture and Design pp. 214–15; Lab Architecture Studio pp. 218–19; Qixin Architects and Engineers pp. 220–21; Jan Siefke/Michael Graves & Associates pp. 222–23; Fu Xing/ XWG (Beijing Tsinghua Architectural Design & Consultation) pp. 224–25; Michael Portman/John Portman & Associates pp. 226–27; Cheng Su, Yang Chaoying/Beijing Institute of Architectural Design pp. 228–29; Architecture & Design/Wood and Zapata pp. 230–31; John Portman & Associates pp. 232–33

The publisher has made every effort to trace and contact copyright holders of the illustrations reproduced in this book; we will be happy to correct in subsequent editions any errors or omissions that are brought to our attention.